Exploring Writing and Play in the Early Years

Exploring Writing and Play in the Early Years

2nd Edition

Nigel Hall and Anne Robinson

David Fulton Publishers
London

David Fulton Publishers Ltd
The Chiswick Centre, 414 Chiswick High Road, London W4 5TF

www.fultonpublishers.co.uk

First published in Great Britain in 1995 by David Fulton Publishers.

Second edition published 2003
10 9 8 7 6 5 4 3 2 1

David Fulton Publishers is a division of Granada Learning Limited, part of
the Granada Media group.

British Library Cataloguing in Publication Data
A catalogue record for this book is available from the British Library.

ISBN 1 84312 010 0

Typeset by Textype, Cambridge
Printed and bound in Scotland by Scotprint, Haddington

Contents

Preface

This book started off as a booklet. It was originally conceived as a report on a curriculum project with which we had been involved for two years. However, the opportunity arose for this to be published in book form and it seemed appropriate to make our coverage of the topic wider and more extensive. We have now been given the opportunity to revise the first edition and take account of some formal changes in education that have taken place since the publication of the first edition.

Our changes seek to do several things. The first is to acknowledge that since 1995 the National Literacy Strategy and the Curriculum Guidance for the Foundation Stage have appeared and do make a difference to how classrooms and settings can operate with literacy and play. The second is to offer more practical advice for those who want to develop or extend the play and literacy provision within their classrooms or settings. We are well aware that many people now working with young children are not qualified teachers or nursery nurses and may not have had experience of creating and organising socio-dramatic play. The third is to extend the exploration of literacy and play by adding a new chapter. This sets up a more extensive background for the case study in Chapter 5.

We have a long list of acknowledgments to make. So many people have helped in preparing this book. First, we are pleased to acknowledge the funding received from Arjo Wiggins and The Royal Mail which enabled us to carry out the work which forms the second half of this book. This work was to explore how young children can get experience of writing non-chronological texts in play and project situations, and we particularly focussing on how this could be done using letter writing. Chapter 5 demonstrates how useful letter writing can be. In our work on this project we were so ably assisted by Sally Brassington, without whose competence and diligence little would have been accomplished.

We must also thank all those schools and teachers who allowed us free access to their classrooms and their children. Our intrusions must have interfered with daily life and we appreciate their willingness to put up with our visits and demands. We must particularly mention Sheila Sidebottom and the staff of Hazel Grove Infants school, now alas no longer in existence. For several years they allowed us to wander into their school, watch them teach, and talk to the children. We have never seen such a dedicated, informed and successful group of teachers and we wish them all well in their future careers. It would be remiss of us not to give special mention to one teacher in particular, Beverly Booth, who was the teacher behind the work reported in Chapter 5. We are confident that anyone reading that section will share our admiration of teaching of the very highest quality. We can only hope that our reporting of her work does justice to her skills.

We would also like to thank the many students and teachers whose work has in small or large fashion appeared in Chapters 2 and 3. These include Sue Endicott, Carol Field, Helen Dutton and Louise Quinn. We hope we have acknowledged all of it, and apologise should we have missed anyone out. We must also thank friends in the US who have been supportive of our efforts to think about play. We thank Kathy Roskos, Susan Neuman, James Christie and Billie Enz.

Finally, but certainly not least, without a very large number of children there would have been no book. Like their teachers they have been prepared to have us walk into their lives. At all times they have received us with friendship, with courtesy, and with dignity. These children have taught us that while they may be young, they are not without wisdom, generosity and immense ability.

CHAPTER 1

Play and writing: an overview

Introduction

If twenty years ago anyone had carried out a thorough database search looking for articles about the topic of play and writing, the searcher may well have found almost nothing. They could have found many thousands of articles about play and almost as many about writing but, as the saying goes, 'ne'er the twain shall meet'. Play was play and writing was writing and the two did not disturb each other. Equally, if one went into a range of early years classrooms there would be play areas and there would be reading and writing activities, but they were quite distinct and separate activities. Play was *only* play whereas reading and writing were *work*.

In 1985 a group of teacher education students and their tutor (Nigel Hall) set up a home corner in a small nursery school and not only put in it all the conventional artifacts of homes, such as cookers, pans, tables and so on, but also filled this 'home' with relevant print-related materials (see Hall *et al.* 1987). They then sat and watched as the four-year-old children got stuck into their play and into the use of the literacy materials. This work was publicised through conference presentations and later articles. One of these presentations took place in London at the World Congress on Reading and the presentation was to be made by the students. After it, Nigel received a letter from a very experienced early years adviser. She told how she was in the room and when she realised it was 'only' students, she thought she'd move to another session. The room was so full that she could not actually get out, so she sat there feeling somewhat disgruntled. She wrote that after about five minutes her position had changed. Suddenly she was thinking, 'How on earth have I been an early years adviser for so many years and failed to think of doing this? It seemed so obvious when the students described what they had done.' This was most people's reaction to the work – why had they not thought of doing something so obvious. Why this might be so will be explored later in this chapter, but one of the impacts of this research was that play and literacy became partnered in many early years settings. So much so that four years later when the British National Curriculum was introduced play and literacy were formally on the agenda.

In the second version of the *English in the National Curriculum* documentation (DES 1990: 35) the Programmes of Study for Writing, Spelling and Handwriting contained the statement, 'Pupils should write in a wide range of activities. Early "play" writing, eg. in a play house, class shop, office or hospital, should be encouraged and respected.' The Non-statutory Guidance stated (p. C14), Classroom areas with materials for writing within practical activities, and role-play areas, should be carefully planned. Here children can practise recently learned and emerging skills whilst watching and talking with each other, as well as responsive adults.' For the first time play was related to literacy in a curriculum document that carried immense political weight. Teachers of children aged five to seven were encouraged to build literate play areas and teachers working with younger children could do the same knowing that this activity had official sanction. It was, of course, too good to be true and when the curriculum was revised, not by a panel of literacy experts but by a group of three special political appointees, all references to play disappeared. It was as if play had become a four-letter word that should not be uttered in polite educational company.

Things were to get even worse towards the end of the 1990s when the National Literacy Strategy emerged and the later document *Framework for Teaching* appeared. It was not the absence of any mention of play that was so problematic, after all, many teachers had wisely continued to encourage literacy-rich socio-dramatic play provision in their classrooms and settings. The problem lay in the structure imposed and its implications for time. The framework document formalised whole class teaching as the main means for teaching literacy and imposed a very highly structured and compart-mentalised pattern (the 'literacy hour') on the teaching, both of which were backed up by heavy-handed official inspections from the Office for Standards in Education (Ofsted). While the Framework was not and is still not mandatory, it took a very secure school to depart from its stipulations when Ofsted might be appearing round the corner. When this was combined with the numeracy strategy and the other demands of the National Curriculum, teachers not surprisingly claimed that play, and of course literacy-related play, had to go because there was no time available on the timetable. While the framework was directed at children in formal schooling it had its impact upon children's play and literacy in nursery settings. The top-down nature of schooling meant that many felt obliged to be preparing children for life in a world of literacy and numeracy hours, and many settings for younger children became much more formal in their teaching methods, cutting back on rich socio-dramatic play provision.

However, not all was lost and in the year 2000 the Foundation Stage cavalry came chasing over the horizon. Not only did the Foundation Stage lay claim to the education of three- and four-year-olds but also claimed the reception class containing the five-year-olds. With the *Curriculum Guidance for the Foundation Stage* (QCA 2000) play was restored to the early years curriculum. Indeed, so important is it considered that a page was given to proclaiming its importance, and it started with (p.25), 'Well-planned play, both indoors and outdoors, is a key way in which young children learn with enjoyment and challenge.' This of course was a claim about play in general rather than specifically about socio-dramatic play, but it was, nevertheless, very welcome to early years practitioners. But what about socio-dramatic play and literacy, and especially writing?

In the introduction to the section 'Communication, Language and Literacy' the phrase 'role-play' occurs only once on the first page in a fairly general statement:

> To give all children the best opportunities for effective development and learning in communication, language and literacy, practitioners should give particular attention to:
>
> giving opportunities for linking language with physical movement in action songs and rhymes, role play and practical experiences such as cookery and gardening. (p.44)

On the second page, play is given its own highlighted paragraph:

> In play, children are given the chance to imagine and to recreate experience. As they explore situations, events and ideas, for example building with blocks or making a journey on vehicles, they improve their competence with language through social interaction, repetition and consolidation. Language is developed further and links made with literacy if, for example, in the above types of play, children are also encouraged to look at maps and plans and relevant reference books. As they play, children will practise doing and saying things that they are not really able to do, such as making a journey into space. They can capture their actions in drawing, early writing or painting, and retell events to friends, practitioners and parents. They are learning that pictures and words are symbolic ways of preserving meaning.

On the third page, the one focussing on teaching strategies, we first find the claim that:

> Children are more likely to write as part of purposeful play.

and further down the page:

> Demonstrating the use of language for reading and writing will be through telling stories and sharing books in a clear and lively way that motivates children. It will be through encouraging children to read and write in a variety of play and role-play situations that match their interests and stimulate dialogue, activity and thinking.

Given that this is a general introduction to communication, language and literacy, one can hardly expect specificity, and certainly within the above comments are a range of central but very generalised ideas about play and literacy. However, only a couple of them really pick up on the relationship between play and writing, so one needs to turn to the specific section on writing (pp.64–7). The document devotes two double-page spreads to writing in the Foundation Stage, one of which is devoted solely to activities designed to aid the development of writing recognisable letters, in other words, handwriting. Yet suddenly on this page the practitioner is presented with one idea about play: 'Provide opportunities to write purposefully by, for example, placing notepads by phones or making a reservation list in a cafe.' On the other double-page spread, which appears to be about making meaning with writing, there is an example of what children might do: 'Marcia is playing in the cafe and writes customers' orders on her notepad. She tells the chef, "they want pizzas."'

It is, of course, the case that the whole area of communication, language and literacy is a huge one, and that for young children oral language will start as the dominant mode of communication and hearing things read to them will follow in significance. However, it is worth comparing not only the number of pages given to the respective topics, but also the amount of text on each page of the section on writing with the amounts that almost seem to overflow some of the pages on oral language and reading. It is as if the authors of the document were struggling to find enough to say about the topic and this feeling is reinforced by the generality and vagueness of what is there, and the utter failure to seriously indicate anything about how children might progress in their understanding of writing. It is not surprising that the richness and power of what becomes possible by linking socio-dramatic play with literacy, and particularly writing, fails to be presented in this document. It is as if there is still a reluctance to acknowledge that young children's understanding of the nature, function and use of writing can be dramatically changed by linking it with socio-dramatic play. The rest of this chapter starts to explore why this relationship is so important.

Play in early years education

Historically, British schools, from the inception of state schooling, were work dominated. However, since the end of the nineteenth century, play has had quite high status throughout Europe among advocates for early years education. There is a long list of notable educators and researchers who have stressed the value of play for the development of children. Research has indicated that play is important physically, socially, intellectually, linguistically and emotionally. As a consequence, early years education (3–7 years) adopted more and more an approach which utilised play in all its manifestations. Even so, although play was not excluded from classrooms, it did tend to be restricted to the early years. It usually disappeared once children reached the age of seven and the demands of schooling became more formal.

Despite that adoption of play by educationalists, play was, and to a large extent still is, viewed by society at large as a non-educational process: it was all right for very young children and all right outside of school. But school, it appeared, was for learning not playing.

In the US a different kind of psychological approach led to a work and testing dominated curriculum, even with the youngest children. It was generally only in the preschools and kindergartens that play established itself. Even here it appears to be under threat. A US writer, Partridge (1988:8), says 'true play seems to have given way to formal learning as zealous parents "push" their children to achieve', and a survey of 103 preschoolers, their parents and teachers carried out by Rothlein and Brett (1984) found that the majority of parents did not support the idea of a large amount of time for play in preschool. One of the major reasons for this was the feeling that children needed to spend more time on academic work. It seems that the many positive messages about play from people who have studied it have, so far, been less than convincing.

This has certainly been the case in the UK where in the late 1980s one Secretary of State for Education penned several pieces in national newspapers to complain about young children doing too much play and too little work. He felt children in school needed to be made to work, not made to play.

The disinclination of parents to accept that learning can take place through play was nicely captured by the novelist Timothy Mo in his book *Sour Sweet*. When the son first goes to school his Chinese mother is aghast when he tells her what he has been doing all day.

> She couldn't believe what Son dropped in an aside: that they played with plasticine and flour and water in class-time. He had been doing that at home for years.
> 'Bad to tell lies, Son,' she admonished him gently.

However, later, when the son is needed to help serve in the shop, she discovers that he has no difficulty in working out the money involved. She finds it impossible to accept that he learned through play.

> 'Ah Mar-Mar, we play buying things at school in play-shop with plastic meat and pretend-money'.
> 'Clever boy.' Kiss. 'But bad to tell lies, Son.'

Play is a rather wide term, and students of play have so far failed to come up with a definition about which they can all agree. Play does cover a rich and diverse range of behaviours. However, in this book we are concentrating on one type of play – 'socio-dramatic' play. The term 'socio-dramatic' may be new to many teachers. It is essentially play in which the participants take on roles, either purely symbolically or semi-realistically. In the UK it has often been called 'structured play'. However, the label 'structured' is confusing, as many different kinds of play can be structured – water play, sand play etc., and anyway, it tended to be used to imply that it was the teacher doing all the structuring. Almost all play is structured in some way and a lot of it is not done by teachers.

Even the term 'socio-dramatic' is not without its problems. How exactly does it differ from other activities in which participants take on roles? When exactly does socio-dramatic play stop being 'play' and become active learning, project work, simulation, drama, theatre, imagination and even 'reading', for reading has been described as 'at root a play activity'? (Nell 1988) In this book we are not going to get bogged down in arguments about definitions. We prefer to leave our, and teacher's, options open. As one of us wrote in an earlier book, 'If we become too precious about the significance of differences in definitions of play, then we are in danger of neglecting possibilities which transcend the formulation of precise categories (Hall and Abbott 1991).

Perhaps three-year-old Suzy-Anne gives the simplest indication of what we mean by 'socio-dramatic' play:

Suzy-Anne: Will you play a game with me?
Anne: Yes, go and get one.
Suzy-Anne: No, I don't mean one in a box, I mean like being people.

(Suzy-Anne aged 3.5 years

'Being people' does not always require the actual presence of other individuals.

Ben's gait was the hop, skip, and jump – proof enough that his heart was light and his anticipations high. He was eating an apple, and giving a long, melodious whoop at intervals, followed by a deep-tones ding-dong-dong, ding-dong-dong, for he was personating a steam-boat. As he drew near he slackened speed, took up the middle of the street, leaned far over to starboard, and rounded-to ponderously and with laborious pomp and circumstance, for he was personating the 'Big Missouri' and considered himself to be drawing nine feet of water. He was boat, and captain, and engine-bells combined, so he had to imagine himself standing on his own hurricane deck giving the orders and executing them. (From *Tom Sawyer* by Mark Twain)

However, Ben did need to conceive of himself in relation to other people. They were implied rather than actual. 'William' had problems with the actual:

'Play houth, William,' said Violet Elizabeth eagerly. 'Ith suth a nith game. You an' me be married.'
'Red Indians an' you a squaw?' said William with a gleam of interest.
'No,' said Violet Elizabeth with distaste, 'not Red Indianth.'
'Pirates?' suggested William.
'Oh no, William,' said Violet Elizabeth. 'They're tho nathty. Juth a nordinary thort of married. You go to the offith and me go thopping and to matineeth and then to the dinner and that sort of thing.'
('William the match maker' from *Still William* by Richmal Crompton)

Life in play is like life in general, not always a bed of roses.

Traditionally, socio-dramatic play has, in Britain, been seen as something owned by children. When it occurs in classrooms, children are usually left on their own to get on with it. Teachers may have a role in determining the overall structure of the area (e.g. Dentist, Three Bears' cottage, etc.) and may be influential in resourcing play areas. However, once the structure is ready, the children have the responsibility for organising themselves within the play setting. Although teachers may intervene because of excessive noise or local disputes, on the whole when teachers enter the play area it is to play with the children. They take on the children's agendas; they sit drinking tea in the kitchen, or get their broken arms bandaged in the doctor's surgery. Allowing the children ownership of the play may not be solely a recognition of its important cognitive benefits. If children can sort themselves out during play then teachers are able to concentrate on other pupils. A truer picture of the valuation teachers put upon play might occur when statements are heard like, 'You can go into the play area after you have finished your work,' or by experiencing classrooms where play occurs only in the afternoons after the 'real' work has been done in the mornings. Whatever the reasons for the existence of play, the advantages for us are that by allowing children to 'own' their play, it retains real power in their minds.

When children play they live their parts. Paradoxically, there is nothing so real as the unrealness of socio-dramatic play. Children engage with an intensity often not matched by their involvement in other areas of classroom life. Perhaps that is why many adults find it so threatening – they are jealous of children's apparent power to escape from the problems of real life. There are two issues relating to this view. The first is that children do not escape the problems of real life when they play; to some extent it is their way of handling the problems of real life. The second is that, in their own ways, adults too create fantasies in which they engage with terrific passion. Indeed, socio-dramatic play has been legitimised for adults by precisely the people who often object to it being carried out by children. A form of socio-dramatic play is frequently used by commerce and industry to train and educate the highest levels of their workforces. However, it is not called play – it is called simulation. Somehow it is all right for adults and three-year-olds to play out various roles but it is illegitimate for children in schools.

It is part of the rationale for this book that the educational attributes of socio-dramatic play more than justify its inclusion in the educational curriculum. It is the word 'play' that is part of the problem. Maybe teachers of young children should try using the term simulation and see whether it makes a difference to the way parents view the activity. A teacher in Yorkshire wrote to one of us to recount an experience. She was working with four-year-olds on the 'three little pigs' traditional story and, in connection with this, they had set up an estate agency (real estate office) in the classroom. One of the grandparents came in, looked at the estate agency and said, 'I don't know what thee'll teach these nippers wi' that'. The teacher and the grandchild gave the grandfather a tour of the area and explained what was being learned. At the end, the grandfather proudly said, 'I think thee's a clever lass!'

Literacy in early years education

School learning is centred around literacy. A main focus of schooling is learning to read and write, and most other bits of schooling depend heavily upon being literate. The control of most literacy education by teachers has been a consistent feature in the last hundred years (Hall 1987). The influence of behaviourist psychology resulted in literacy being seen almost solely as a visual/perceptual skill, and one which was highly individualised. It resulted in learning experiences being structured in carefully controlled systematic sequences which atomised and segmented learning. It demanded the decontextualisation of learning, the reading and writing of meaningless material, and the isolation of the learner. Ironically, above all, it required the de-skilling of learners; children had to ignore everything they knew about learning and submit the ownership of their learning to teachers, publishers, and university academics. The consequence was that the process of learning literacy became very complex, ritualised and, for the most part, utterly divorced from either pleasure or reality. Many children failed.

Given the way school literacy learning was defined, it appeared somewhat bizarre to look for literacy learning prior to schooling. The small number of children who did turn up on the first day able to read conventionally were sufficiently abnormal to be the subject of detailed study by psychologists (Torrey 1979). The rigidity with which many teachers stuck to their sequences meant that the literacy abilities children did possess (and sometimes they were very high levels of ability) were often ignored, or remained unknown. Literacy was something that very definitely had to be taught; and where was one taught? – in school.

It was not until the mid-sixties that inroads began to be made into the rigidity of both the teaching and the understanding of literacy learning. For the first time new definitions of literacy opened up new ways of thinking about it. If one viewed knowledge about literacy as not solely about knowing a restricted set of sound–symbol relationships, but as having some under-standing of what literacy was for and about, then literacy learning clearly did not start once children went to school. If knowing about literacy is knowing about why people use literacy, where they use it, when they use it, what they use it for and who uses it, as well as how it works, then children are learning about literacy well before formal schooling. If one perceives literacy as an object of the world rather than of schooling and asks, 'How do children come to have knowledge of "significant" objects in the world?', then it becomes possible to see the emergence of literacy as something truly developmental, as something intellectually constructed and controlled by children, and as something beginning long before formal instruction occurs.

The key word is 'significant'. If children ignore print and see it as quite insignificant, then it may be the case that children's attention would have to be drawn by teachers to this phenomenon. But do young children see print as irrelevant to their lives?

We live in a very complex environment in which print plays a major part. That environment makes an intricate set of demands upon those who interact with it. It necessitates substantial involvement of almost all who live within it. It is virtually impossible to live within it and be unaffected by print. The speedy advent of modern information technology has, far from reducing the burden, added to the complexity of print-related life. One consequence of the complexity and demand for involvement is that children are, from birth, witnesses to both the existence of print and the relationship between print and people. It would seem somewhat strange, given the way children involve themselves in all aspects of their world, if anyone suggested that there was one part of that visible world about which children were totally ignorant. Yet, as has already been pointed out, that is precisely what educationalists have done.

Ferreiro and Teberosky (1983:12) put it most clearly after they had searched the literature on literacy:

> We have searched unsuccessfully in this literature for reference to children themselves, thinking children who seek knowledge, children we have discovered through Piagetian theory. The children we know are learners who actively try to understand the world around them, to answer questions the world poses . . . it is absurd to imagine that four or five year old children growing up in an urban environment that displays print everywhere (on toys, on billboards and road signs, on their clothes, on TV) do not develop any ideas about this cultural object until they find themselves sitting in front of a teacher.

The evidence of recent years has been that those 'thinking' children are there busily making sense of the world of print. This 'sense' is not, of course, the same sense held by teachers. The evidence of a multitude of studies reveals that children are intensely interested in the object that we call print, are curious about it, and are constantly puzzling out why it is there and what it does (Baghban 1984; Bissex 1980; Cochran-Smith 1984; Crago and Crago 1983; Dyson 1989; Ferreiro and Teberosky, 1983; Goodman, Y 1984; Harste *et al.* 1984; Heath 1983; Hubbard 1989; Kammler 1984).

When Ferreiro and Teberosky (1983) studied young Argentinian children and asked what kind of sense are children making of literacy, they were not concerned with whether the children were right or wrong. They were interested in the beliefs, and the constructs and concepts that the children actually held. For Ferreiro and Teberosky print is an object of knowledge just like any other object or set of objects in the world. Just as children develop knowledge hypotheses about how things move, why some things fall to the ground, why some things float, why people get angry, so they generate ideas about how print works.

Ferreiro and Teberosky claim that in normal circumstances children do not sit passively waiting to be told what they should learn, but simply get on with learning by operating upon the world. They learn by having a go, by trying things out. Early childhood is a continual process of experimentation, risk taking and negotiation, in purposeful, intentional ways, and providing that children are growing up in a print-rich environment then those strategies will be applied to generating knowledge about literacy.

There is now overwhelming evidence that this is so (Hall 1987). In the process of observing reading and writing, young children are involving themselves in a huge range of situations in which literacy appears. The consequences of this discovery can be seen clearly in the UK National Curriculum where even the youngest children are expected to have experience of a rich range of forms of text. It is also evident in the many books from the United States about Whole Language teaching, that children's use of literacy in its widest sense can be encouraged and nurtured.

Play and learning about literacy

It was quite a while before researchers and teachers began to see how play and literacy could come together. Curiously, although many educators were interested in both play and literacy, few saw them as critically related topics. How could play be related to literacy when play was something that started early, was a seemingly natural event, did not need teachers and was never associated with failure, whereas literacy had to wait until children were aged five or six, had to be taught, took a long time to learn and was associated with quite a lot of failure?

However, it ought to be clear from what has already been said that while literacy and play were conceived of as totally different objects, some similarities were emerging. It was now possible to view both play and literate behaviours as under the control of children. It was possible to see in both that children engaged with a rich variety of world experiences and knowledge, rather than limiting themselves to those things conventionally seen as appropriate to children. To be young was not to be without means of engaging with the world in all its complexities.

It is at precisely that point that the potential relationship between play and the emergence of literacy comes into sharp focus. It has been well established that socio-dramatic play is almost always a process of 'experimentation, risk-taking, and negotiation, in purposeful, intentional ways'. If it can operate like that across a multitude of social and intellectual experiences can it not operate in the same way for the emergence of literacy? Indeed, the question might better be, 'Does it operate like that?' There is a growing number of studies that have explored the dimensions of both those questions.

Some researchers have argued that there is a very straightforward relationship between play and literacy. Gentile and Hoot (1983:436–7) suggest, for instance, that through painting children become aware that 'images on paper are meaningful and say something' and claim 'movement activities also provide children with vocabulary and conceptual growth by allowing them to

giving ⓐ chance to attain skills.
+ exemplify that these 'marks' are relevant - by making their own are learning how
important it ⓒ ⓑ to make marks of real meaning - want others to share in their (articles)
writing ability / ability to form meaningful marks!

discuss body parts and positions'. More specifically, a relationship is claimed with reading: 'It is difficult to imagine how a youngster might possibly read and abstract meaning from a sentence "John went into the box" if she had not had the concrete experience of crawling in and out of a real box.' Thus the relationship is a very general one. The connection between play and literacy is to some extent incidental, as precisely the same kinds of relationship could be established between play and many other cognitively demanding activities. Play, in this instance, is being used simply to denote a physical activity that provides a concrete experience. The relationship is between play and the content of literacy rather than between play and the processes of literacy.

At a more fundamental level Bruner's work has been extensively directed to examining the relationship between play and the acquisition of a symbolic system like oral language. He claims that, 'It is not so much instruction in either language or thinking that permits the child to develop his powerful combinatorial skills, but a decent opportunity to play around with his language and to play around with his thinking that does the trick' (Bruner, 1986: 81). Developing literacy means coming to grips with a second-symbol system. Isenberg and Jacob (1983:272) claim that, 'Symbolic play, the process of transforming an object or oneself into another object, person, situation, or event through the use of motor and verbal actions in a make-believe activity, provides an important source for literacy development.' It does so because both play and literacy involve handling words in such a way as to represent objects, ideas, or actions. The work of both Piaget and Vygotsky suggests that this ability to handle symbolic systems has immense potential for facilitating literacy development. However, tracking this relationship at such a general level has proved difficult.

Galda and Pellegrini (1985:vii) claim that 'The language used in play is similar to more formal, literate uses of language required of children in school'. This argument seems a refinement of the more general claim by Scollon and Scollon (1981) that children in Western literate societies are inevitably encultured into ways of using literate language because the language structures of the communities in which they live derive from an 'essayist' culture rather than an oral culture. Thus the Scollons were able to say that, at two years of age, their daughter Rachel was effectively literate as she was already using language structures, aspects of which were inherently 'literary' rather than just oral.

There seems to be a curious omission when most of the previously mentioned studies are examined. It appears that very few people had considered the relationship between play and literacy by giving children the opportunity to play with literacy-related objects in situations where using literacy would be an appropriate response. Hardly anywhere, in the studies mentioned so far, does one see children playing at literacy. Whyever not? It seems obvious that if you want to study the relationship between play and literacy then you put children into situations where they are able to demonstrate what they do when they play with literacy. In other words, give children contextualised play situations where they can demonstrate what they know about the 'what', 'why', 'when', 'where' and 'how' of literacy.

Play offers an opportunity to help children develop this wider understanding of literacy by allowing them the chance to explore literacy in contextualised situations. As indicated above, this relationship between children's play and emergent literacy has hardly been examined.

Isenberg and Jacob (1985) observed two four-year-olds engage in play in a literate environment. They found that 'Both girls engaged in playful literacy activities at home and in school'. They offer extended reports of the girls engaged in 'veterinary' play. Isenberg and Jacob comment, 'Both four-year-old girls engaged in playful literacy activities in pretend and non-pretend play contexts, activities that seemed to involve two functions related to learning: the gradual incorporation of the new information into the children's behaviour patterns with the formation of larger units of behaviour and the elaboration and extension of known or familiar information to new contexts' (p.20).

Bessell-Browne (1985) examined specifically the nature of the use of literacy in socio-dramatic play areas in kindergartens. She was able to identify ten types of usage. These were (with examples):

- as an oral language substitute (mark-making followed by an explanation of the message)
- as a source of information (using the cookbook for ideas)
- to extend and explore personal relationships (sharing feeling about animals while looking at a book on pets)
- for self-expression (to express sorrow at a death in the family)
- to confirm identity (writing their names on everything and anything)
- to present information (writing captions)
- to support memory (list-making)
- to meet economic and business needs in their play (ordering from catalogues)
- as models (copying names from labels)
- to reflect the official status of an activity (writing carefully because it was 'important work')

Bessell-Browne was able to record that the literacy-related resources were used by almost all the children and were used, for the most part, in an appropriate and typical manner. She commented, 'Children used literacy in a variety of ways that were meaningful to them in the play setting. They also showed knowledge of many of the ways adults use literacy in the wider social context and incorporated this into their play indicating a developing understanding of the many uses of literacy in the real world. The children's spontaneous literacy play thus gave them an opportunity to extend their uses of literacy beyond those that may be generally encountered within a classroom' (p.155). Thus whatever kinds of literacy instruction were present in that classroom, the children had, in their socio-dramatic play, the opportunity to learn about and to explore a valid and wider perspective on literacy.

Both Bessell-Browne (1985) and Schrader (1985) made some use of Halliday's categories of language functions (Halliday 1977). Bessell-Browne used it to guide her in the provision of appropriate literacy-related resources while Schrader (see also Chapter 3 in this book) used the categories to examine the written language functions of children's writing during play. Schrader commented that:

> The children demonstrated their developing knowledge of written language functions not only by writing for real-life purposes but by reading their writing and discussing the meaning of their written language with their classmates and teacher. The children's actions further verified the meaning intent of their writing. (p.59)

Roskos (1988) reported on her study of the reading and writing behaviours in the natural pretend play of children aged 4 and 5 and said, 'I came away awed by the quantity of early literacy activities in the pretend play context' (p.562). She was able to log 450 reading or writing acts for eight children within the periods of her observation. She claims that, 'In putting literacy to work in their play, these youngsters behaved like readers and writers. They assumed a literacy stance and in so doing exposed their theories-in-use about the functions and features of written language' (p.563).

Hall *et al.* (1987) set up a play situation in which literacy was an embedded feature in order to see whether children made any use of the literacy-related objects. For their investigation, the 'home-corner' was subjected to a 'print-flood'. By the cooker were placed cookery books, recipe pads, a recipe note book and writing utensils. Similarly throughout the home-corner, related and appropriate literacy materials were provided. It was felt important that a wide range of print-related resources was provided, particularly with the writing utensils, for as Harste *et al.* (1984:34) reported:

> Children at three know that usually pens are used for writing and crayons for drawing. In fact when Joan asked one of her three year olds to write with a crayon, her young sophisticate said, quite matter-of-factly, 'No I need a pen'.

The home-corner also received a desk area with paper, envelopes and writing utensils. Newspapers and letters were pushed through the door before each session. In addition, diaries, planners, telephone directories, books, catalogues and other print material were placed in strategic places.

In this area, and with these resources, the behaviour manifested by the children demonstrated a keen commitment to literacy. During the four days of observation 290 events in which literacy-related behaviour was exhibited were observed. These ranged from fleeting bits of engagement to highly organised and sustained episodes of play in which literacy was a consistently embedded feature.

On occasions the children seemed to be exploring the materials in very personal, non-play ways. In one event a young boy was told by one of the girls involved in some family play to read the newspaper. There then followed a five minute solo engagement (the girl had gone away) in which the boy manipulated and manoeuvred the paper until he had sorted it round to the correct orientation and then he sat and gave it the most intense scrutiny. It was as if he was not only exploring the orientation of the newspaper (which, being the *Guardian*, was a large object for him to handle) but exploring also the role of being a newspaper reader.

In the same way, the children in the nursery school demonstrated not simply a knowledge of some of the purposes of print but of the social contexts in which these purposes were embedded. Inevitably the range of understandings displayed was limited, but it is clear that there are a range of functions which are quite comprehensible to the children. Children do experience greetings cards, thank-you cards and letters, lists to Father Christmas, menus, advertisements for favourite products, packets with familiar foods, shopping lists and, of course, stories.

The children displayed a very wide range of mark-making intended as writing. It was clear that the experience of the children in using print was quite varied. The results were often unconventional but were nevertheless a demonstration of how much had been learned already; a demonstration that would have been impossible without the appropriate resources and the opportunity for display.

The children in this nursery group were exploring the use of written language to establish ownership and identity, to build relationships, to remember or recall, to request information, to record information, to fantasise or pretend, and to declare. Those children were not waiting for formal schooling to use literacy but they had been waiting for the opportunity to display their use of it. The play situation generated within the classroom allowed these four-year-old children such an opportunity.

Since then a number of studies have explored the consequences of making play areas into areas properly resourced with relevant print. All have reported that the children actively explored the print in ways that showed clearly their interest in, and knowledge of, its functions and purposes (Neuman and Roskos 1991; Roskos 1990; Roskos and Vukelich 1991; Neuman and Roskos 1992; Neuman and Roskos 1993; and see also the chapters in Christie 1991, and Roskos and Christie 2000).

Writing and play

In this chapter our journey has been from the separately conceived areas of play and literacy to a point of view which sees them as having a range of possible relationships. To a large extent the move towards writing and play is, in a straightforward sense, impossible. So much of what has been mentioned in the previous section was as much to do with reading as it was with writing. We would admit that although the rest of this book focusses upon writing, so much of what we have to say involves as much reading as writing. However, we feel that despite this there is so much to say about play and writing that a whole book is needed.

The function of this short section is to introduce our theme rather than to explicate it. The rest of this book is our explication. It also a chance to use a few examples that would fit less comfortably into other sections. For instance, could anyone writing a book about the relationship between play and writing conceive of the one picked out by Arthur Ransome? Ransome wrote one of Britain's best known children's books, *Swallows and Amazons*, although its age, and some political incorrectness, mean that it is, these days, probably more heard of than read. However, for many, many years it was one of Britain's most popular works of fiction for children. In later years Ransome was persuaded by his publishers to write a short biographical pamphlet. In it he explained how he started his writing career:

> I was a cheerful, small boy of action rather than of letters. Then one day we were playing at ships under and on a big dining-room table which had underneath it, in the middle, a heavy iron screw pointing downwards. It was my 'watch' below, and brother or sister was on the bridge, on top of the table, and suddenly raised a shout for 'all hands on deck!' I started up, and that big screw under the middle of the table made a most horrible dent in the top of my skull, altered its shape and so, in one moment changed my character for life. I crawled out, much shaken; and that very afternoon wrote my first book about a desert island, in a little notebook with a blue cover. I have been writing ever since.
>
> (From 'The life of Arthur Ransome' by Hugh Brogan)

No doubt we could refer to that as starting one's writing career with a bang – but we'll avoid the temptation! While it is tempting to suggest that teachers arm themselves with heavy tables containing an iron screw, we suspect that doing so would produce a writ rather than a writer.

In the chapters that follow we are going to consider the relationship between play and writing in three different ways. In Chapter 2 we consider the extent to which play can be considered as authorship. We look at the ways in which children create scripts for their play and show that the act of composing in play has many important relationships with the act of composing in writing. This is perhaps a more complex chapter than the ones that follow; it is, however, a very fundamental one for our book.

In Chapter 3 we examine how writing can often occur within the action of the play. When resources are available during play, children will use them. There is no finer example than that provided by Richmal Crompton who, more than most writers, managed to get inside the heads of young children. William and the Outlaws have decided to adopt an orphan. The problem was where to find one. The answer was to turn to literacy and write a notice:

'Well, let's spell it all the ways it could be spelt, so's if one comes along it'll know we want one.'

Douglas therefore drew up a fresh notice whose final form was:

orfun

awfun

wanted an

orfon

awfon

They fixed it on the barn door and gazed at it proudly.

'Well, one's more likely to come along if we aren't here, waiting for it to come,' said William. 'Things never happen when you're waiting for them to happen. I votes we go out to look for one and then I bet you anything that when we come back here we'll find one waiting for us here.'

The outlaws recognised the sound sense of this and set off. As they were setting off Ginger looked doubtfully back at the notice.

'I bet he won't think much of us not knowin' how to spell it', he said.

Douglas returned and wrote slowly and carefully at the foot of the notice:

'WE GNOW WHITCH IS WRIGHT'

(From 'William adopts an orphan' in *William-the-Bad*)

In Chapter 4 we revisit the relationship between writing and play but do so at a more theoretical level. We consider in some detail what it means to use literacy in everyday life and compare this with how it is used in schooling. We then move to exploring how socio-dramatic play shares a number of elements with everyday contexts for literacy and in particular examine the notion of events.

Chapter 5 takes the ideas of Chapter 4 and explores how they could operate in practice. Most of this chapter is a case study of how a group of five-year-old children used literacy not to learn about literacy but to achieve a range of purposes that were related to a major play experience. Each of these purposes involved different ways of using written text and we show how the children coped with exploring their knowledge of written language to influence and inform other people.

Finally we will overview our chapters and sum up our case for linking writing with play.

CHAPTER 2

Play, writing and composition

When young children are asked to write, they often respond by saying, 'I don't know what to write'. On the other hand, it is extremely rare for children to say, 'I don't know what to play'. If you leave a couple of children together, they start playing. If there are a few props lying around they utilise them in constructing their play. At first sight it appears that writing and playing are different kinds of activities. Clearly one is done with a pencil or other marker and is manifested by putting words on paper so that they seem relatively permanent. The other seems relatively free flowing, formless and ephemeral. There is, however, one very important and fundamental similarity between the two activities. Both are about creating texts. In this chapter we want to explore the extent to which composing a text during play is similar to composing a text with written language.

When young children engage in socio-dramatic play much of what happens occurs through talk. Let us look at an example. At first sight this episode has no connection with writing; the children do not use print in any way whatsoever:

Anthony:	There's the fish, the fish is coming.
Natalie:	Is it a baby one? Is he a new baby one?
Anthony:	Give it some ice-cream.
Natalie:	Is it a baby one?
Anthony:	Oooh, shall we help her?
Marina:	Pretend that's a shark, pretend it's a shark.
Anthony:	Oh, a shark, help! Quick, quick!
Natalie:	You say, 'It isn't a shark'.
Anthony:	It isn't a shark.
	Pretend I'm going fishing. I need that, it's my sword.
Natalie:	Here's your crisps.
	Who wants this? It's some power.
Anthony:	I've got some power.
Natalie:	We'll do some fish stew for your supper. I'll make it out of this.
Anthony:	Get that fish out of here.
Natalie:	It's one of them fish there. You say, 'It isn't'.
Anthony:	It isn't.
Natalie:	It is. You say 'Oh yes it is 'cos one's gone'.

Anthony:	Yes it is 'cos one's gone . . . Oh no it isn't, it's the one I gave you.
Natalie:	No it isn't, just pretend.
Anthony:	I've killed my wife.
Natalie:	Karl, you come in and say, 'He's killed her'.
Karl:	He's killed her!
Anthony:	Guess why? 'Cos you know that fish I gave her, she was killing it. She was terrible.

There are two important uses of talk to be seen in this episode. There is the talk which constitutes the dialogue of the characters in the play. It is that talk which allows us to learn about what is happening in the narrative. In other words it is the talk which constitutes the on-going story of the play. Then there is the talk which regulates the play. It is that talk which allows us to see how the narrative is being composed and organised. In the above extract it is the talk like 'pretend that's a shark' and 'you say it isn't' which contributes to the regulation and control of the narrative and the behaviour of the characters.

One way of looking at this would be to see the play text as a script in which the content is the dialogue spoken by the characters and the other bits are the directions to the characters. Another way of looking at it would be to see the content as the story, and the other bits representing the reflective activities of the composer or composers.

What happens in each type of talk? In the talk which constitutes the dialogue of the play, the children: realise their characters; follow the agreed script; sustain themes in their text and reveal changes in the direction of the narrative. In the talk which regulates the play, the children: step out of character in the narrative and into the role of author ('pretend that's . . .'); develop roles for characters ('Karl, you come in and say . . .'); transform the plot ('Pretend I'm going fishing . . .'); and keep characters on task ('No it isn't, just pretend').

In the process, children shape and develop the text of their play. These authorial comments can fulfil a wide range of functions. Garvey, in looking at the social nature of play, identified a range of what she termed 'framing statements'. Children use these structures to:

- Define the situation
  'Let's play house.'
- Assign roles
  'I'll be the daddy and you be the mummy.'
- Define the location
  'This can be the kitchen.'
- Specify the action plan
  'I'll fix supper for the kid and you get the groceries.'
- Assign props
  'This is my purse.'
- Correct operating procedures

'*Girls can't be doctors.*'
- Refine the performance of others
    '*No, you have to really yell at him.*'
- Invoke rules from 'reality'
    '*You can't really go out there.*'
- Terminate or shift the story
    '*Ok, supper's finished; what do you want to play now?*'
- Clarify relationships
    '*We're playing so we're friends now, right?*'

Garvey saw these functions as part of the mechanism for maintaining the play and the social relationships of the participants. In other words, such defining statements were part of the glue that held the bits of the play together. Of course they do serve this function but we want to go a step further and claim that such statements are powerful evidence for considering play to be authorship. They are manifestations of intellectual moves that all authors of fictions make but which are usually hidden from the readers of a written text. They are manifested in play largely because such play often involves several children and therefore planning and organising has to be made explicit. From our point of view this accident has the beneficial effect of making the authorship process visible.

In other words, we are privileged to hear the children engaged in explicit and negotiated decisions about the text they are creating. When we hear such parts of play, what we are witnessing is the mutual composition of a narrative text. The composition is happening in action rather than simply inside a writer's head. Just as composing a piece of complex story writing involves a number of intellectual, authorial moves, we wish to claim that so does composing a complex piece of socio-dramatic play. Thus, although the above extract had on the surface no relationship to writing, in fact the process by which the text of the play was generated, and manifested and controlled is highly literary, and is very similar to the processes by which authors create written narratives.

On a very general level there are similarities between the texts created in play and the texts created in writing. Forbes and Yablick (1984) claimed the task of framing in fantasy play literally becomes: 1. Constructing a scene; 2. Populating it with characters, and 3. Bringing it to life with action. This does not happen by accident. That the action subsequently occuring often has a story-like quality can be seen clearly in a piece of play observed by Roskos (1990). The play is about visiting Sea World and seeing the killer whale called Shamu. She felt able to divide the text into three fairly fundamental aspects of narrative.

The Beginning (setting, purpose and characters)

S: I'll be right back, Dad. [*He walks over to Emily.*] Would you come with us? Let's go to Sea World.

E: Sea World! Let's watch Shamu! I'm the mom. [*All three children run to one end of the room and sit down next to one another. They gaze towards the other end of the room.*]

The Plot

S: Oh! I see Shamu.
E: It's starting.
A.J. Yeah!
E: There's a little fish. There's a big mom.
S: There's a daddy.
E: Look! He fell on the ice. Look at 'em. Mommy and Daddy are fell! Oh-h-h-h-h.
S: Oh-h-h-h-hh Baby Shamu slipped. Let's go see 'em!

Resolution

[*The three run to the other side of the room.*]
S: [*Patting a pretend baby Shamu.*] Oh-h-h-h! I know you're all right. [*All three make stroking motions on a pretend baby Shamu.*]
E: Look! All better now. [*She pretends to lift Baby Shamu back into the water; the boys assist. They then run to the other side of the room.*]

Very young children are the composers of complex narratives long before they can make conventional sense with the marks that constitute writing. We would like to look more closely at three of the important compositional moves made by both child players and authors of written texts.

A vital and early authorial decision is to determine what the text will be about. To put it another way, 'What will we play?' This is, of course, the equivalent to saying, 'What shall I write about?' The answers to such questions are seldom easy ones. Some authors of written texts will tell you that they don't know what they are going to write about; that it sort of develops once they put things on paper. Indeed, it was E.M. Forster who is reputed to have said, 'How do I know what I am going to say until I've written it?' However, this is being somewhat disingenuous, as Forster elsewhere reveals that before he physically began to write *A Passage To India*: 'I knew that something important happened in the Malabar caves, and that it would have a central place in the novel – but I didn't know what it would be.' That short quote shows that Forster knew he was: (a) writing a novel; (b) had situated his novel in a particular location, and (c) knew that there was to be a major event at some point. Clearly some major authorial decisions had already been taken and those decisions both constrained and freed the development of his narrative.

Children have to make certain decisions when they start to play. These decisions might have to be made from scratch, or they might be influenced by particular events, resources, places, experiences or stories.

The extract below is from an episode in which a group of four-year-old children had been allowed for the first time to play in a space which had been fitted out, and labelled by the teacher, as an office.

Emily   Pretend you're one of the visitors.
Laura   Yeah.
Emily   Go on, go out there.
Laura   Pretend I'm a helper. Yeah.
Emily   Pretend you're the . . . pretend you're the person that comes to open the bank.
Laura   No, pretend, I er . . .
Emily   Was helping me, yeah.
Laura   No, let's pretend I'm a helper.
Emily   Yeah, you could help me . . .
Laura   I know this could be where the aeroplanes come in, and . . . and . . .
Emily   This could be the office of the aeroplane.
Laura   Yeah, that's what I was going to say.
Fiona   It's open now, isn't it.

The problem for the children was that 'an office' was a fairly novel concept for them. Deciding what to play in this new and interesting environment was not easy.

You will notice that the talk here is all what we called above, 'regulatory talk'. The topic or situation of the forthcoming play text is being explicitly negotiated. The children need to find a topic about which they can all feel happy, which is likely to be satisfactory, and to have some scope for development. Anybody who has tried, even in a modest way, to write fiction, will know just how important these things are. The principal difference between play and written texts is that children's play texts are usually constructed by a number of players while a written text tends to be authored by a single person. However, of course, children do create solitary play texts (see the Laurie Lee example later in this chapter) and authors of written texts do sometimes collaborate (as in the authorship of this book).

In the extract above, the children are looking for a script which they can all feel has some potential for development. The theme is gradually being established and this leads to another crucial authorial move.

If the children are to successfully play together then there needs to be agreement, of sorts, about the kinds of things that can happen during the play. It would not make much sense if every child conceived of each theme or topic in a totally unique way. The play would simply fall apart and there would either be no play, or very incoherent, probably parallel, play.

Cooperative play works because not only do children negotiate topics but because the topics they select have features known to the children and which lend an overall structure to the play. In the previous example we could see the children trying to find a 'script-type' in which they could use the resources of the office.

What do we mean by a script-type? Some psychologists who study play have termed what goes on in play as 'scripted' behaviour. They do not mean that it has a written-out script as in a play in a theatre; they are using script in a more schematic way.

For French *et al.* (1985) a script is:

> A schematic representation of events and includes information about temporal and causal organisation of a set of related acts, about which components of an event are obligatory, and which are optional, and about the props and roles associated with the events.

You can see what happens when psychologists get hold of an idea! However it is less complex than it seems. They are saying that scripted play has an underlying structure and built into this structure is information about the who, when and what of the play. Within any one script certain things are allowed to happen and certain things are not.

To any one who has recently come across genre theory, this definition has a familiar ring to it. In genre theory a genre is often defined as 'any purposeful, staged, cultural activity in which human beings engage'. You will notice that both the word 'script' and the notion of 'staged' have a literary 'ring' to them; the choice of metaphors is rather interesting and significant in seeing play as a piece of composition.

What both definitions are about is that certain activities have an overall shape or pattern, and that this pattern influences or determines other elements of the activity. In both play and writing, the decisions that authors make about the overall shape of the piece or play have many consequences for how the ensuing 'story' is composed.

As we have already seen, the first decisions that most children make when playing, and most authors make when writing, is what the activity is going to be about. Are they going to play hospitals, mummy and daddy, Little Red Riding Hood, etc.? Are they going to write a story about a witch, a set of instructions for making tea, or an argument for voting for the Monster Raving Loony Party? Whatever is chosen, there will be an event pattern, or script, or genre. In fact the way we recognise certain activities is that we can identify them through their patterns. For instance, we recognise a sales encounter by certain stages in the action, certain players, and certain relationships between the players and so on. A typical pattern in a sales encounter in a more traditional shop might contain:

an entrance into a shop,
a greeting,
a request,
a response (positive or negative),
if positive the handing over of the goods,
the passing over of money,
an expression of gratitude
and an exit from the situation.

We could say either that there is a script for a buying event or that there is a genre called 'buying'. It is schematic. It covers many different kinds of buying events and can to some extent be modified and yet still be recognisable as a 'buying' event. Scripts exist for this situation, and breaking the script causes problems. People in the UK might remember how *The Two Ronnies* used to be particularly good at exploiting what happened when the shop scripts were not played out correctly. In fact some of our most famous comedy sketches have creatively explored this genre; need we say more than, 'This parrot is dead'?

Do young children know this basic script, or genre?

M: Hurry up I'm on my way to Manchester.
F: Don't nag – want a fork? Big or small peas?
M: No peas, fish and chips love.
F: Salt and vinegar?
M: Yes, lots and lots, loads – leave 'em open.
F: Five pounds please.
M: Gosh they're cheap today! See ya.
F: Bye love.

These were four-year-olds. Don't they know the script! Look back at the definition. The script is the underlying structure. There is announcement, an invitation to buy, a request, procedural transactions, request for money, and an exit accompanied by social niceties.

In the same way that these four-year-olds know the script type, so when authors set out to create a certain kind of text they understand the rules of the genre. Thus if you set out to write a detective story, you know it needs certain kinds of characters, certain kinds of events, and a certain kind of style. There are many different detective stories but we still recognise them all as detective stories. Of course, some authors experiment, mix genres, play around with our expectations, but the success of such moves depends on the readers already knowing the genre and being interested in the challenge to their expectations.

To sum up, once children have decided what to play, their knowledge of the script enables them to generate some kind of structure around which to develop their play. Of course, not all children do this, and as teachers and parents we know what happens. The other children come running up complaining about the child not playing properly.

In the incident in the fish and chip shop, the filling out is relatively easy as the script is (a) a well known one, and (b) follows the basic script pattern very closely. It is highly structured and little negotiation was needed in this instance. This is partly indicated by the fact that there was no regulatory language needed in that extract; the story could get on by itself.

Now the important thing is that these scripts can be strongly contextually bound or they can be weakly contextually bound. In the strongly contextually bound situation the children's freedoms are considerably less. Thus, if they choose to play fish and chip shops then a lot of strong elements tend to influence the play. However, children still create variations on the script.

Here is another segment from the same play:

M: Close the shop, no more food!
L: Can we have two beefburgers and chips?
M: No, we're closed.
L: No you're not, your sign is open.
M: There's no food, just chips.
L: We want those two beefburgers there.
M: Oh, OK. Then we're closed.
L: Thanks Mr Fish-man. We want chips with them.

Essentially the same underlying scriptural features govern the action, but the children create different scenarios based around the scriptural structure.

Some scripts are highly contextually bound. If the children choose to play out a traditional story, say Little Red Riding Hood, then a whole mass of things tend to be highly prescribed. On the whole, so long as you are playing Little Red Riding Hood, the wolf has to be bad, and has to lose. So whoever plays the wolf has to lose. If a wolf refuses to die , then again, the cry is likely to be, 'John isn't playing properly'.

Such highly structured scripts can impose limitations on the way children play. Superhero play is based upon models that are so very limited, restricted to a very basic plot, and contain very black-and-white characters. The creative aspect seems to be little more than choosing what character to be, and then going 'pow' and 'zap'. This does not mean that all superhero play is bad; it has some powerful things going for it (see Paley 1984), but it may be capable of less extension, as children often feel disinclined to change the basic parameters of the story line.

Where pre-existing scripts are less clearly defined (and there are almost always some constricting elements) then the children's creative role in developing the script becomes a more powerful one. They become less like authors who retell stories and more like authors who create original fictions. Characters have to do things, actions need to proceed, the story has to be kept going. If children are to transcend the constraints of generic scripts, then they need to be able to generate individual texts within the script-type.

Authors of original fiction have the capacity to use imagination to act creatively on the texts they develop. If the wolf decides not to die we might have children running to the teacher with complaints but we might also have a sudden dramatic turn in the play.

When in play one child steps outside the narrative and says to another child, 'Karl you come in and say "He's killed her"', then the other child somehow knows that it is an invitation from a co-author to transform the text. As authors, children have the freedom, indeed the power, to: transform their texts; lift them out of the conventional; experiment; take risks; and to imagine. The four short extracts below show how a dramatic suggestion can suddenly shift the direction of play, but at the same time be instantly accepted by the other players:

A: It's your grandmother fallen in the deep river.
K: I'll rescue her, come and help me.

D: I'll be the pirate and get the treasure.
A: We'll throw you over.
D: Help, the shark's getting me!
K: OK, we'll get you.

K: The spaceship's on fire
N: When you hear this sound..'na na na na' it means the spaceship's on fire

D: Aliens. One's killed Ben.
A: The Space Invader will get it. Go on Space Invader.

These are not huge transformations but they did change the plot in each of the episodes recorded. Invitations were accepted in each case without any hesitation. And so, with the help of the imagination, the text progresses.

Invitations to transform are not always accepted:

Boys playing 'turtles' arrive in the play area:

C: You're not playing the turtles down here, you've got to go upstairs and play.
D   We are the real turtles.
C   Well, we're cooking, we'll burn ourselves if you shout, so play upstairs.
D   No, but we're the real turtles don't you know?

In this piece from Paley (1984):

Andrew: Can we play?
Charlotte: Yes, but don't make a noise. The baby is sleeping.
Jonathan: We're aliens. Take one more step, I'll shoot you.
Mary Ann: No. You have to say 'Pretend we have babies.'
Paul: We're the babies.
Mary Ann: No. Say 'Pretend we have babies.'
Paul: I'm a wild bronco.
Andrew: You be Big Hulk. I'm Little Hulk.
Jonathan: I'm the pet dinosaur. Pretend I'm scaring the girls.
Mary Ann: Get out! Only the girls are scaring people. You can't play. Out! Out!

[The boys leave uncertainly but without protest.]

In similar ways as a written text progresses, so ideas will be generated, some rejected, some incorporated; some work and some don't. The authorial process is one of constant refining. The book the author ends up with is usually rather different from the idea they started with. The play the children end up with is usually somewhat different from the idea they started with. In both cases a story is being told. The children are creating a story. They are the authors of the play. It is clear that the creation of a socio-dramatic play text is surprisingly like the creation of a written fictional text. The main difference is that at the end of one there is a product, at the end of the other, a memory.

The relationship of play to fictional text creation is also apparent where oral storytelling is concerned. Carol Fox (1993) studied the oral stories of a group of children. She felt able to claim (p.25):

> The children's stories of this study are forms of verbal symbolic play. There can be no doubt about that as one listens to the tapes. As they narrate the stories the children show their pleasure in their own inventions; they mock, laugh, joke, exaggerate, sing, whistle, make strange noises and give their characters funny voices. They invent worlds peopled by lions, bears, rabbits, monkeys, witches, giants, robbers, policemen, heartless mothers and small children. They make literal use of magic and coincidence, extreme forms of punishment, a great deal of violence and much fear and suspense.

What is clear is that most children, when learning to write, already know a great deal about how to construct texts. The problem is that too often the trials and tribulations of learning to hold pencils, writing letter shapes, and rendering sounds into symbols create a distance between learning to write and being able to compose. However, some teachers have managed to utilise this relationship between play, composition and writing to help children cope with creating written texts.

In *Cider with Rosie*, a semi-autobiographical account of children by Laurie Lee, there is an episode in which the central character, a boy named Tony, is playing by himself one evening:

> 'Tony was playing with some cotton reels, pushing them slowly round the table. All was silent except Tony's voice softly muttering his cotton reel story.
>
> '. . . So they came out of this big hole see, and the big chap say Fie and we said we'll kill 'em see, and the pirates was waiting up 'ere, and they had this gurt cannon and they went bang fire and the big chap fell down wheeee! and rolled back in the 'ole and I said we got 'em and I run up the 'ill and this boat see was comin' and I jumped on board woosh cruump and I said now I'm captain see and they said fie and I took me 'achet 'ack 'ack and they all fell plop in the sea wallop and I sailed the boat round 'ere and up 'ere and round 'ere and down 'ere and up 'ere and round 'ere and down 'ere . . . !'

Just as Tony was using the objects to create a play script which could subsequently be written down, so one teacher we know, Julie Morley, uses this technique quite specifically to help the children compose written text; a process she calls 'storymaking'. In her classroom, pairs of children use small props, often miniature people and animals, to create and play out a story. They know that when they have done this, either they or the teacher will write their story down. Thus the connection between the play text and the written text is very explicit. Julie's belief is that the compositional aspects are so similar that playing first makes the writing both easier and more successful because the children are not having to compose from the start when they put pen to paper.

To begin with the children simply explore the props; they then set about the task of creating a story. As they play they are consciously composing, and this provides the chance for the teacher to listen to what is happening. Storymaking allows the children to represent symbolically their real or imaginary narratives. The children are not restricted by their physical writing skills as they have the option of taping or dictating their story, only writing it if they wish. At various times in the activity the teacher can intervene. In the first instance she may set up the topic or basis for the story. It is sometimes related to the topic being studied in the class (in the example below it was part of a study about the history of the Industrial Revolution. The class had been on a visit to Ironbridge, where the very first iron bridge in the world was erected and still stands.) This teacher believes that children need to base their writing on experience even when the writing is to be imaginary. They incorporate into their stories experience of hearing stories, reading stories, real life, discussions and interactions with both teacher and peers.

L: 'Help! Help!'
M: I saw them so I jumped down.
L: 'Help! Help!'
M: You shouldn't be doing that.
L: Being naughty.
M: 'Tend this one sneaked to the mine . . . 'tend they sneaked to the mine.
L: To where the dad was working . . . where the dad was working . . .
M: 'Dad can we help?'
L: He says no.
M: And they made them fall . . . these two . . . these two make themselves fall into the mine. 'Hey, we have to find the children.'
L: 'Oh, no, I hope they're not down the mine . . . Go and check . . . I'll go down.'
M: 'Oh, no, they're in the mine.'
L: 'tend they let themselves lower the . . . down.
M: Yeh, but they get out just in time.

Having played out their story, the teacher came and talked to them.

L: So it can be a storybook and we can keep it in the reading area and I want you to write it down.
T: But you have to work out what it's going to be first and then I'll write it down.
M: When you are writing it we'll tell you.
T: Let's think what you've got already. You've got the coal mine.
M: The coal mine.

T: And you think there's going to be an explosion.

M: And the house.

T: And you have to decide what the children were going to do, 'cos you said the children were in it before . . . are they going to be in it?

L: They were outside looking at the people working.

T: Oh you think they are going to be watching?

L: To see where there's an explosion then they run away.

M: That was the mountain . . . the high cliff. If the children fall that means the coal mine has to go down very quick.

L: The coal mine is very long and has to go down there and there's a candle touching . . . the candle makes it very hot.

T: Right, you carry on. Work out what the story is going to be . . . then I'll write' it down.

In this instance the play is turned into story. In the work of Vivian Paley the writing is turned into play. Paley developed a technique which at first sight seems the reverse of what is described above. She works with kindergarten or younger children. She collects from the children oral stories which she writes down for them. Later the children act the stories out. Now the notion of 'acting out' is a bit different from most of the things that we tend to think of when we think about socio-dramatic play. But we are not sure that the difference is as great as it first seems.

The children in the 'chippy' were acting out a well experienced, and maybe previously played, scenario. Most superhero play is based on plots taken directly from explicitly presented stories. Children who play out fairy tales or well-loved books are relying heavily on pre-existing scripts. Indeed, for Paley that reliance is what makes the acting out work so well. She says in Wally's stories (1981:122):

> The printed story, whether by an adult or a child, promises dependability. The soldier will always kill the witch; the lost child will invariably find his parents; everyone will live happily ever after.

For Paley, play is, anyway, often based on well-experienced sources (1988:12):

> The children were actors on a moving stage, carrying on philosophical debates while borrowing fragments of floating dialogue. Themes from fairly tales and television cartoons combined with social commentary and private fantasy to form a tangible script that was not random or erratic.

Paley's technique was to have children tell her stories, which she wrote down. Later a child had the opportunity to act out the story. The child would choose who played the characters and often amend the story in the process. As the story was acted out, so the audience and other players observed, made comments and raised issues. The stories became much more complex narratives as they were acted out. Although this process seems the reverse of almost everything above, it is, of course, a continuous process. These stories were being dictated and acted out every day. Paley (1981) points out that 'As the year went on so the stories the children wrote became longer, more clearly structured, and more complex as the experience of acting out the story fed back into the composition of the writing'.

She later comments:

> Before, we had never acted out these stories. We had dramatised every other kind of printed word – fairly tales, story books, poems, songs – but it had always seemed enough just to write the children's words. Obviously it was not; the words did not sufficiently represent the action, which needed to be shared. For this alone, the children would give up their play time, as it was a true extension of play.

And she indicates its relationship to socio-dramatic play by saying, 'Their stories resembled the informal dramatic play that went on all day and received the same kind of intense concentration'. Paley makes explicit for the children a relationship between the act of playing and the act of writing.

So far in this chapter we have considered the general but important relationships between authoring and playing, and have also briefly looked at two specific ways in which teachers have linked play to the authoring process. In all the above instances the act of playing is separated from the act of writing. However, it is important to note that as many children embark on authorship so they play as they write. This may be in the sense of being playful (Daiute 1990) but it may also be in the sense of manifesting the action to aid the composition as it occurs. A number of writers have commented on the ways in which young writers link their writing with drawing, or even use their drawing as the text of their stories. The work of Rowe (1993), Dyson (1989), Hubbard (1989) and Paley all relate to this oral accompaniment to drawing and composing. Paley (1981:5) said, 'If I insist that the boys sit down and draw, they animate their volcanoes and space wars with exploding noises, as if they have jumped inside the picture.'

Everything in this chapter indicates that it is appropriate to consider socio-dramatic play as authored text. It involves negotiating settings, creating characters, and having these characters engage in various actions within events. Like young children's story writing, play tends not to be planned composition; it is very much created as it develops. It is also clear that there are some positive ways in which teachers can explore these relationships in the classroom.

Singer and Singer (1990) suggest that socio-dramatic play becomes internalised as people grow up and lives on as a strong component in our imaginations. Thus, if we have an interview the next day, we tend to lie awake all night imagining the action of the interview. We use our ability to role play in the head to try out a range of texts in the hope that they approximate to the reality of the next day.

How do authors of written narratives develop the capacity to create characters full of life, who interact with each other in a range of interesting ways? Could it be that internalised dramatic play has a large part in helping authors develop the capacity to achieve richness of narrative? An author has to get inside the heads of characters and imagine lives as they might be lived by the characters. Perhaps early experience with socio-dramatic play is an important component of achieving this later in life. After all, that is what children do when playing. As Weininger (1988:144) says:

> Pretend play, it seems to me, is a special category of play that involves a child's understanding and representation of reality. It is, in effect, a 'what if/as if' situation. For example the child thinks, 'What if I were a firefighter? What would I do?' The child thinks about this for a while, assembling the bits of reality known about firefighters derived from storybooks, the comments of adults, observations of real life and television. The child first imagines what being a firefighter would be like and how it would feel to be one, and then plays it out 'as if' he or she were one. To the best of his or her ability, given the factual knowledge of reality and the availability of props that can be used in the 'as if' situation, the child says and does what he or she has imagined a fire fighter does.

Planned composition requires anticipation, and experience of what happens when characters interact in certain kinds of settings. Where better to gain some of that experience than within socio-dramatic play? It seems that might have been how the children's author, Enid Blyton, learned to construct her stories, first by being a player, then by imagining the action and characters and eventually by writing it up. In her biography (1986:53) she wrote:

> The games I played were much the same as yours, of course – Red Indians, Burglars and Policeman, Making a House somewhere – behind a bush, or up a tree, or under a table.

and then later:

> When I went to bed I used to lie still and wait for my 'thoughts'. I didn't know what else to call them then. I suppose now I would say that I waited for my 'imagination' to set to work . . . What were the stories about that came into my mind? There were stories about myself, of course – I did brave deeds, I remember, in my 'thoughts'. I had many adventures, the favourite of which was being wrecked on an island somewhere and having to do as Robinson Crusoe did and make a home for myself. (p.61)

One can almost see the Famous Five and the Secret Seven emerging.

Putting it into practice

The evidence of Chapters 1 and 2 shows clearly that young children need very little support to engage in socio-dramatic play. They can convert any item into a powerful symbol and invest it with character and physical attributes. Put one child into a room with another and before long some kind of socio-dramatic play will emerge. However, it is possible for adults to provide powerful support for children's socio-dramatic play, help generate a greater variety of play and even help some children understand cooperative socio-dramatic play. Such help may not only benefit children as players, but also facilitate deeper understanding of narrative.

Modern views on the development of young children's authorship (Kress 1997; Pahl 1999; Lancaster 2001) make it clear that very young children author texts using whatever is available to them and whatever seems most efficient to them. This authorship might often look as if it has nothing to do with conventional print-related authorship. But all authorship is essentially about making meanings using symbolic systems, and print is only one of these, albeit one that has been given immense significance in contemporary education systems. Children author texts (and not just narrative texts) through using words orally, through singing, through drawing and painting, through collage, through modelling, through print-related marks, through socio-dramatic play, and of course, through combinations of all of these. Storying in any of these modalities has the potential to inform the others. It is very important that teachers do not treat these above modes as separate areas of the curriculum. So link socio-dramatic play with these other forms of meaning making. This can occur before the play and themes carried across to the play, or play could be followed by multi-modal explorations using music, modelling, writing, drawing, etc.

The immense pressure upon teachers and others who work with younger children often makes it easy to leave play alone while seemingly more important work is carried out with other children. However, the evidence suggests that play is a very powerful tool for teachers learning about children. However, to learn about them from their play it becomes important to create space and time to observe and listen. There are no simple answers to the problem of finding time to do this but we think it is important enough that teachers or other adults in a setting do set aside a small amount of time for learning about and even participating in children's socio-dramatic play. It may be that tape-recording or, even better, videoing could be used to capture parts of play. Time spent by teachers and other adults in observing play will increase their ability to understand what is going on, and the more skilled one becomes, the less time is needed to gain information of value, especially for record keeping.

Adults could find a simple checklist helpful in observing play. Who plays and how often? Who contributes regulatory talk and acts like the director? Who initiates creative twists in the play? Who has a good sense of narrative and uses it to move the play along? Who cooperates efficiently with the other players? Who brings important world knowledge to the play?

As we have already observed in this chapter, play is authorship in action but usually there is only a memory of the play as a legacy. This seems a waste of a powerful activity, and while we would not want to suggest that all children's socio-dramatic play is taken over for curriculum purposes, taking some space and time to reflect on or extend the attributes of play can be beneficial. Tape-recording, videoing or even simply photographing small parts of play can create opportunities for all the children to look at and reflect on play. Children watching the images or listening to the voices can ask questions and the original players will have to respond. As well as creating challenges for the players, such discussions can often extend other children's understanding of what is possible in play, creating a model for less experienced players. Teachers could invite children to retell the story created in their play and either invite them to write it down, if appropriate, or scribe for them. It would be possible to modify Paley's technique and have some play reconstructed live in front of the whole group.

The most critical point is to have some of the play text available for scrutiny and revisiting. When working with a children's book, a text can be looked at over and over again, each revisiting yielding more complex thoughts. Exactly the same process can operate with play, so long as there is an accessible video or tape-recording. However, too often when stories are read and reread, the exploration that takes place immediately afterwards involves little more than remembering the plot – the set of 'What happened then?' questions. The book is often set aside while the children carry out this memory game. What such activities fail to do is get children exploring how an author/illustrator has created his or her effects by using words and pictures.

Some time ago we constructed a list of useful ways to examine authorship, and given our claims that socio-dramatic play is authorship in action, it should be no surprise that many things on this list work as well with images of play as they do with books. This list is written in the language of adults. Teachers and others must use their professional judgments about what to discuss and how to phrase the points they choose. The list is a repertoire of possibilities, not a checklist for a session. Select one or two things to discuss as there will always be another time to pick some of the others. Do not expect too much from young children and do not try to lead them to your own idealised responses. It is always much more rewarding and informative to listen to what the children have to say.

What happened in this play?
> How did the players pattern and sequence their text? How were the significant moments in the plot indicated? How did the players create twists and turns to keep the play interesting?

What was this play about?
> What clues were available for us to identify a theme? Was there more than one theme in the story?

Who was in the play?
> How did we find out what kind of characters they were? How did our knowledge of the characters grow? What words, actions and props helped us understand the characters?

Where was this play happening?
How did the players create a sense of place? How much did they tell us about the place? Did the play use real or imagined places? What props helped create this sense of place?

When was this set?
In what time period was the playing set? Was it a fantasy time period? Could it happen today or tomorrow? How was the time period indicated by the players? How did the players convey a sense of passing time?

How does this play make you feel?
How did the players engender feelings in the viewers? What words, phrases, sentences or actions aroused those feelings? How did the players create effects like fear, horror, revulsion, sympathy, etc?

What does this play make you think about?
What issues in the play make us stop and think? What positions do we take on these issues? How did the players influence us to take a particular position on an issue in a play?

What does this play assume you already know?
What did we bring to the play when we watched it? What do we already know about the subject of the play? How is this play like or not like other plays/stories that we know?

The primary aim of these points is to help the children focus on the nature and structure of the play in which they have participated or are watching. It tries to help them look more closely at what was said and performed – in other words the text of the play. Used with children's books these questions perform a similar function in always taking the children back to the ways in which an author or illustrator has created their effects.

We suspect it is relatively rare for children's socio-dramatic play to be used in this way, but believe the impact of such activity could be considerable. The points raised in the questions above go right to the heart of being a critical reader and viewer; they invite deeper levels of reflections about spoken, written and performed texts and they lay an immensely powerful foundation for the development of fully literacy. Exploring these questions will make for more reflective and more aware learners. Such activities take time, but they are immensely powerful in challenging and developing children's thinking about what they do when they play. They continue to develop children's understanding of narrative and continue to create opportuties for adults to understand the lives and worlds of children.

CHAPTER 3
Writing as a spontaneous event in play

While play is itself rather like the act of composition, and thus all socio-dramatic play has a relationship with the act of writing, some play events seem to invite actual writing.

Margaret Atwood describes such an event in 'Cat's Eye', her wonderful fictional account of a young girl growing up:

> We play school. Grace has a couple of chairs and a wooden table in her cellar, and a small blackboard and chalk. These are set up underneath the indoors clothesline where the Smeath underwear is hung up to dry when it rains or snows . . . Grace is always the teacher, Carol and I the students. We have to do spelling tests and sums in arithmetic; it's like real school, but worse, because we never get to draw pictures. We can't pretend to be bad, because Grace doesn't like disorder.

Example 3.1: Fhamida's register

Where better place to find reading and writing than when playing at 'school'. Fhamida, aged 5, made her version of the teacher's register and insisted on calling her register each morning.

But writing also occurs in many situations other than school play. Denny Taylor, the American ethnographer, described in her book 'Family Literacy' (1983:46) the activities of a group of children who had played in a garage:

> They wanted to have a restaurant in Kathy's garage. They sat on the floor of the garage and wrote out menus. The menus were identical. Later that day I found the menus abandoned on the floor of the garage.

> I asked Louise about the menus. She told me of their restaurant plans, explaining that they were going to have red-check tablecloths and that Kathy was going to take the money in the morning while she was the waitress, and in the afternoon, she was going to take the money while Kathy was the waitress.

These children were nine years old. Schickedanz (1984) looked at the home literacy experiences of a number of pre-school children and persuaded the parents to keep a record of the literacy events. Those records reveal a number of instances where the child played in ways that required the use of written language.

> 'She asked me to sharpen her new multicoloured pencils. I did. She wrote various things on her steno pad. That's the one I got her to take to the meetings where I take notes. She had to have one too you know.' (p.12)

> 'She asked me to help her with her diary. She wanted to make one. Like Martha in the George and Martha story.' (p.12)

> 'She got a pencil and she said to my father, 'What do you do all day?' And he said, 'I play golf'. So she said, 'Golf, how do you spell that?' He spelled it for her. Then she said, 'How do you do it?' It was like an interview. I don't know where she ever saw this, whether it was like on Electric Company or what.'(p.16)

In schools, when literacy resources are made available to playing children, they become a vital and sometimes critical part of the play. Many teachers have discovered that children will not only use the resources but will use them in ways that approximate to their use in real life.

Ten years ago it was extremely rare to find a play area which offered props related to literacy. In kitchens young children would have cookers, sinks, pots and pans, cups and saucers, knives and forks, and even heaps of clay or papier mâché food. But one never saw the print-filled items that can be found in most kitchens. Where were the recipe books, the note pads by the phone, the grocery lists, the calendars, the fridge notice-boards, etc? The only print one saw was on the labels on the packets and tins that were sometimes seen on the kitchen shelves. Why was it not there? Probably because teachers thought that children would not use it. Play was for playing and playing is pretend. It is now clear that when appropriate and relevant print-related resources are provided, children do not hesitate to incorporate them in their play.

In the previous chapter we looked at a couple of bits of transcript from the 'Chip shop' play. While those four-year-olds were playing they also took the opportunity to write. At three and four the chances of finding conventional writing are reduced. But that does not stop emergent writers. Here is just one example of a written order at the chip shop:

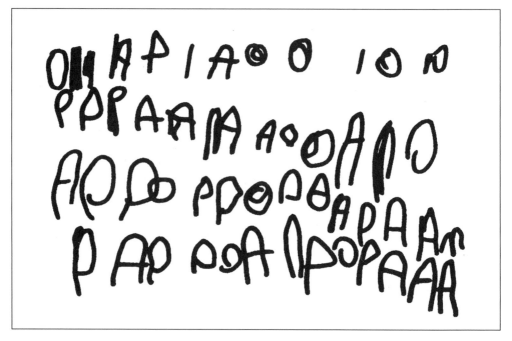

Example 3.2: An order at the chippy

We have boxes filled with pieces of paper which look like this. These bits of paper were once theatre tickets, messages, doctor's notes, receipts, bills, cheques, etc. You name it – we've got it! What is significant is that although the marks may not look like conventional writing they were produced in response to a situation which demanded the existence of writing that performed a particular function. Children in such play demonstrate that they know quite a bit about the nature and purpose of literacy.

We know Example 3.3, below, was a doctor's note because we saw it being used by the doctor in the hospital play. We know that other pieces were theatre tickets because we saw them being given out in the puppet play. Knowledge of writing is not simply a matter of being able to make conventional marks which make conventional sense. Knowing about writing is about understanding when certain types of written objects are needed. Children show at a very early age that they understand quite a lot about the nature and purpose of written

Example 3.3: The doctor's note

language and play is one of the ideal opportunities for them to show it, and for teachers to discover what children know.

Once children are able to write in a conventional way, the writing sometimes becomes more readable. However, the scribbled text is still a typical feature of the play of older children. This may be because it is not important that it is real, simply that it can pass for real, or it might be because a child who has learned to write using print wants their writing to look 'grown up' and attempts to imitate cursive script.

In Example 3.4, below (Dutton 1991), the child could write in a conventional way but chose to scribble. The conversation that accompanied this helps understand it.

Christopher:	Hello. Yes. What's your name?
Emma:	Emma. [*Christopher writes it down.*]
Christopher:	What's your second name?
Emma:	Squigglywink. [*Emma walks off.*]
Christopher:	Hang on! What's your little girl's second name?
Emma:	[Shouts] Squigglywinks! [*Emma giggles and Christopher looks harassed.*]

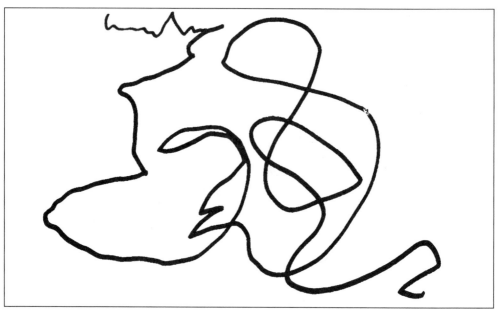

Example 3.4: Just scribble?

When Christopher chose to use 'scribble' to record the names he could hardly have been surprised when Emma responded with verbal scribble. Suzy-Anne produced the piece below (3.5). It is clear from some bits of it that seven-year-old Suzy-Anne can write quite well conventionally. However, she chose to use mostly scribble. Why? Because, as she said, 'I do it like that because I am just pretending to write.'

Several times, we have come across older children who, when being younger children in the play, demonstrated their role-age by using scribble or, even cleverer than that, writing in a beginning writer's script. A good example (and it is school play again) is the following. Christopher is playing the teacher.

Christopher: [*Shouting*] Now children, sit down. SIT DOWN.
Michelle and Ruth: All right teacher.
                     [*Christopher takes Michelle's piece of paper and writes her name on it.*]
Christopher: Watch this. Once . . . upon . . . a . . . time . . . [*He writes 'Once upon a time' on the top of the paper.*] You [*to Ruth*], copy Michelle's paper.
Ruth: Yes teacher.
Christopher: Now you're going to write a story about a horsey and finish the story.
                     [*The girls start writing. Both make their handwriting very large. Their letter shapes are irregular and the content very simple. When asked to read it back, both girls read the pieces in a 'baby' voice, making deliberate mistakes or hesitations.*]

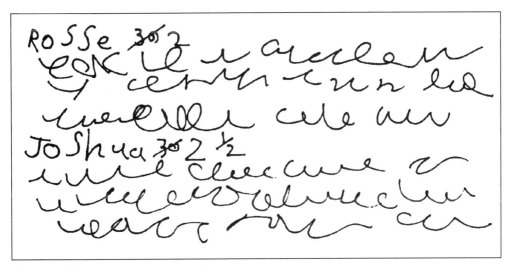

Example 3.5: Suzy-Anne's writing

When children use writing, even pretend writing, in a purposeful way they indicate to us a wide range of knowledge about what writing can do. An American researcher (Schrader 1989) studied the range of writing functions that appeared in young children's play. We have added to her examples some others that we have seen ourselves. Even so, they represent only a sample of what can be seen. Shrader used a set of categories devised by Halliday, which divide language into a limited set of functions (see Figure 3.1).

To put some flesh on these examples we would like to look a little more closely at some of the writing carried out by children in specific settings. One of the most common is the appearance in play of the shopping list. Clearly children have witnessed parents creating shopping lists. They may contribute as did Pauline in this example from Tizard and Hughes (1984). Here, a mother and child are discussing the creation of a shopping list:

M: It's not enough to get all of that, is it? [*Points to list*]
C: No.
M: See! So when daddy gets paid I'll go and get some more money and then I'll go and get the rest.
C: Yeah. That's nice, isn't it mum.
M: Mm . . . I've got one, two, three, four, five, six, seven, eight, nine, ten, eleven, twelve [*counts list*].
C: [*Joins in counting*] Nine, ten, eleven . . . Mum let's have a look! [*Mother shows child the list*] Do it again.
M: We gotta get rice, tea, braising steak, cheese, pickles, carrots, beans . . . oh, Irene's gone to get them [*crosses off beans*].
C: And what's that word?
M: That's lemon drink [*crosses off lemon drink*]. She's just gone to get that one, see.

Instrumental	(*I want*): to satisfy one's material needs, to enable a person to obtain the goods and services needed **Writing a list; writing a cheque; writing an order**
Regulatory	(*Do as I tell you*): to control the actions and behaviours of self and others **Writing plans for future action; writing a sign; writing directions or instructions; writing prescriptions; giving a written warning**
Interactional	(*Me and you*): to interact with others, to participate in social relationships **Writing letters; writing postcards; writing invitations**
Personal	(*This is me*): to express identity and express personal feelings and attitudes **Writing one's name; writing about self; writing a diary**
Heuristic	(*Tell me why*): to explore the world around them, to discover, seek information and solve problems **Writing questions**
Imaginative	(*Let's pretend*): to create a fictional world **Writing a story; writing a poem**
Informative	(*I've got something to tell*): to communicate new information **Writing memos; writing labels, name tags; writing a newspaper; writing textbooks or resource books; writing money; writing name, address, phone number**

Figure 3.1: What do children do with their writing in play?

The above example, and variations of it, are probably common in many children's lives. The event contains a large number of demonstrations about the use of written language. The child is seeing:

- what a particular genre looks like
- a one-to-one correspondence between words and things
- what writing looks like and how it is constructed
- that writing can be rewritten or redrafted
- that writing has a purpose and can be used to direct behaviour
- that writing is a social event
- that writing is tied up with other important areas of life
- that writing is a means to an end.

Of course children do not have to attend to these demonstrations, but it seems that many of them do. Several thousand miles away from Pauline and her mother in the East End of London, were two Puerto Rican children playing in New York.

I: . . . the list. Take the list, Marie.
M: Well. Look, give it to me.

I: All this is the list; all that which is written.

M: Well give it to me little boy; I'll take it. I'll carry it with me . . . the list was pretend little boy.

I: The list is right here. Look at it, it is written.

M: I'm going. Take the list, sir. Now I'll buy the food. Take, take the dollar, I have five left.

I: The list, did you bring back the list?

M: No, they stayed with her; yes, I brought it back, take it.

I: Now it says rice, lentils, soup . . .

M: That is why it cost me . . . this much . . . well, they cost me five dollars.

I: What?

M: Five dollars; things are expensive friend, I don't know why.

(English translation from Jacob, 1984)

There is a striking similarity between the real event and the play event despite huge differences in location and culture. Recently a nursery teacher reported to us some observations of a four-year-old. She and a friend were in an area of the classroom and were talking.

S: Right! I'm writing a shopping list. We're gonna go shopping in a minute, aren't we?

R: I'm doing a list an' all.

S: 5 . . . 6 . . . 7 . . . shoppings. Lettuce and 'nana, Tesco.

R: Yes, Tesco. Yeah! Need 'nanas again.

S: Now, fingers, sauce, erm . . . Lego . . . You all right darling. Darling, what's your name?

R: Mummy!

S: erm . . . chicken . . . 'nana, no not 'nana, rub it off! Oh, I gotta write on back 'chips'. Now, that's me shopping list. Gotta go now . . . go to Tescos, thanks.

The child left the area and went to the brick area. She walked around holding her 'list' and talking to an imaginary person. As she walked she picked up the bricks and put them in her basket, reading her list as she did so.

S: Need 'nanas, lettuce, sauce. Thanks, bye.

For that child, the activity of list-making seems a major part of the play. For a group of older children (six-year-olds) it was merely a means to an end in the play.

C: The shops. Yes, the shops. We go shopping now . . . hey people . . . we're going to the shops.

D: Right, pretend I send you.

C: Yeah! I go to the shops for lots of food.

D: Okay. What do you buy? Pretend we need lots and lots of food and . . .

C: And some cakes.

D: Yeah! And some . . . I know we can buy everything . . . now remember what we need . . . we need . . .

C: I know, pretend to do a shopping list. Shall I do it? Then you won't forget.

D: Mm. You write it down then, 'cause I'm the cook and I . . . and I gotta cook!

C: Okay. S H O P P I N G L I S T (writes it down). Go on you tell me what to write . . . what we need.

Such lists occur fairly frequently in play. Their purpose is often very clear to young children and, as a form of text, they require little skill.

Of course, as children become more experienced writers so writing can be used for many social situations. An ex-student of ours, Helen Dutton, (Dutton 1991) looked at the kinds of writing that went on in a play restaurant being run by six-year-olds. She made the following observational notes.

> Christopher was the cook. Ruth said, 'Do you want a burnt cake? The stupid man put them in again!' David sat at the typewriter and wrote with a crayon on headed notepaper. Ruth wrote a letter of dismissal to Christopher and pretended to strangle him. Christopher appealed, but Ruth told him it was only a warning. Ruth came to me every two to three minutes to complain that various items of food had been ruined by Christopher.

Ruth's first letter to Christopher said:

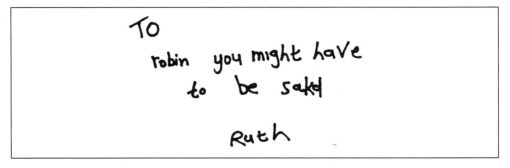

Example 3.6: Ruth's letter to Christopher

It is interesting that she wrote to 'Robin'. It was as if to indicate that he was not to take it personally.

A later fracas led to another letter to the cooks. This time from Emma.

> Dea all
> the cucs we are
> glvelhg You a
> last waning
> lots of love

Example 3.7: Emma's letter to the cooks

And Ruth wrote a much more elaborate text.

> Dear cook
> I Want you to shere the
> Food proply and don't eat
> all the Food up at once
> like a gredy animal I
> whuld like you to be very
> nice to the People that
> some to the restant and
> If you do hot you Will get
> to be sacked and you don't
> Want that to happen do you?.

Example 3.8: Ruth's extended letter

These children were six.

Even teachers can write in play. Another of our students, Louise Quinn, had set up a restaurant in a class of six-year-olds. In her very interesting and significant report she wrote the following:

> One skill which I introduced by becoming directly involved in the children's role play was 'short-hand'. To do this, on one of my visits I took the role of waitress. While in role I observed that Stacey, who was in the role of receptionist, was writing the take-out orders that had been phoned through. She was writing in long-hand.

Noticing how long it took her to write down a take-away order I showed her an order that I had written in short-hand. I had used a mixture of simple pictures and initial letters of words. I asked her if she could work out what I meant by such things as 'sn soup', and 'Cup t' and 'Tof a' She said that this was easy and was able to decode my short-hand very quickly. I asked her why she thought I had done my order in this way.

'Because they're hard to spell?' she asked. I agreed that some words might be hard to spell, especially if I was in a rush and wanted to write down my order quickly. I explained that often real waiters and waitresses used this form so that they can be quick.

'Perhaps you might like to have a go at your own short-hand writing when taking an order over the phone', I said. 'That is what it is called', I explained, 'Short-hand, because you're making the words shorter.'

Next time I took an order from Stacey she had used her own short-hand. Having explained my short-hand writing to all who were involved, I then found that most of the children were able to write using short-hand.

On one occasion soon after this incident, she recorded the following conversation between Darren (the customer) and Paul (the waiter):

Paul: What would you like to eat?
Darren: I would like two cups of tea . . . and soup. Yes, two onion soups.
Paul: Let me see that a minute [*tries to grab the menu*].
Darren: Paul, I'm reading it. You get another.
Paul: I need that one 'cause I need 'onion soups' . . . so I can write it down . . . let me see . . .
Darren: No . . . you're not meant to do it like that. Miss said we can do it quick writing 'cause we can need to do it quick.
Paul: I can't do it quick. Let me see it Darren, I . . .
Darren: You can because Miss . . .
Paul: I can't see it. I'm gonna tell . . .
Darren: Paul, look. Let me do it . . . Pretend I'm not the customer now and then I show you . . . give me the pencil and . . .
Paul: Hurry up Darren, or else we're going to shut.
Darren: Look, this is dead quick, right. Pretend me and him (*a soft toy*) wants two packets of crisps. You can do it like this [*writes 2 p cr*]. '2 p' that means it says 'packets', 'cause it's 'p'. 'cr' that . . .
Paul: That means 'cr' for crisps. 2p cr. Let me have a go. Let's pretend you need . . . you got . . . you need two toffee apples [*writes it down*].
Darren: And two toffee bananas.
Paul: And two . . . do you want two or do you want one?
Darren: Two.
Paul: Two 'tof a' . . . do you want anything else? Yes? Or no?
Darren: Erm . . . No.

Paul: Okay, it'll be ready in about eight minutes.

The effect of this conversation was clearly evident in the order Paul was writing.

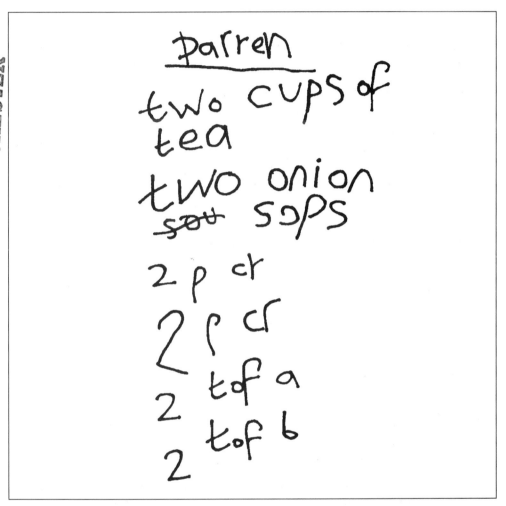

Example 3.9: The waiter's order

When children use writing in their play, there exists the probability that children will be teaching each other for not all children will know as much as each other. Look at this example of two four-year-olds in an 'office'.

[Patti picks up an index card out of a box. Joel also picks out a card; a card that is headed 'J'.]

Joel: Write Joel . . . write Joel on that one. Write Joel, write his name.
Patti: How does your name spelled?

Joel: J O E L
Patti: But does it go up and down?
Joel: I'll show you . . . I'll show you on this 'cos I'm writing on it. [*He turns over the envelope on which he has been writing*] You go like this . . . and this one . . . and then . . . and then . . . like that [writes his name on the envelope].
Patti: Right. Does it go J O L like that . . . Can I draw 'L' instead of all that?
Joel: No just draw all of it. [*Shows her the writing on the envelope and taps it with a pen.*]
Patti: Well let me look at the picture then.
Joel: [*Walks over with the envelope and says quietly*] Eh, that's not it.
Patti: I can't do it.
Joel: I can. See if that one's got a 'J'. I'll write it then with my pen . . . There, J O E L. [*He writes it for her.*]
Patti: Pretend I've done that writing then . . . say 'Thank you for doing all that writing', but pretend.
Joel: Thank you for doing all that writing.

This next example was recorded by Neuman and Roskos (1991)

David: [*to Aaron*] Wanna buy this book?
Scott: [*to David*] This is a library. They don't buy 'em, they rent 'em.
Aaron: Could I rent this book please?
Scott: Do you have a library card?
David: [*to Aaron*] No, this book is not for sale anymore.
Aaron: Are these for sale?
Scott: No . . . you don't buy 'em, you borrow 'em.
David: This is a good book.
Aaron: All right.
David   [*He writes on a piece of paper as if recording the withdrawal.*] You've got four days.
Aaron: 'Kay. Hey, I bought . . . I borrowed this scary book for four days!

In both these instances the presence of writing opportunities in the play allowed children to pass knowledge about literacy on to other children.

When the play is appropriate and the resources are present, children incorporate play in their scripts as naturally as any of the other physical actions that appear in the play. They write tickets,

Example 3.10: A reservation for the Hilton

they use different languages,

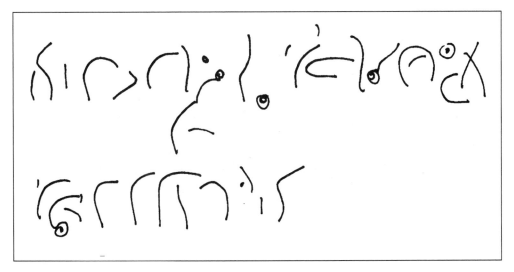

Example 3.11: Four-year-old Kasid's 'Letter'

they signify when their shops are open or closed,

Example 3.12: Four-year-old Leon's sign saying the shop is closed

and even write receipts.

Example 3.13: Four-year-old Joseph's receipt for a pair of 'frog slippers'. (*Frog slippers, sold 30th February*)

While most children's use of writing in their play will be relatively short-lived, it has been known for such writing to have very powerful consequences. We will conclude this section with a mention of what is surely the most famous of all examples of writing occurring within play.

> Between the hours of five and seven they might go and play in the 'nursery' . . . or in the kitchen if it were winter and a fire indispensable.
> This was 'the very witching hour' of the day for them. In it they entered on a life completely different from, yet deeply influenced by, the routine life of the parsonage and their free life upon the moors. It was like a third plane of existence upon which they moved, not as children subjected to the rule of their elders but as deities dispensing Night and Day to attendant multitudes.
> They created for themselves a microcosm reflecting every aspect of public life, political, military, judicial and social. This escapist paradise completed that liberation of their spirits begun by an early and close contact with the natural scene about their home. Like all creations of the spirit it was a spontaneous growth arising, in the most natural manner in the world, out of their games.
>
> (From *Anne Brontë* by W. Gerin)

You will have guessed that the subjects were the Brontë children. Not only did they create this world in their minds but they wrote about it, creating wonderful miniature books recording all aspects of life in this world, books which can today be seen in the Brontë Museum in the Parsonage in Haworth. Perhaps this play and the writing that accompanied it were powerful elements in the subsequent literacy success of the three sisters. Who knows, in our classrooms today there may be equally distinguished future novelists beginning to exercise their imagination by using writing within their play.

Putting it into practice

Building a play area that includes items usable by children for literacy-related behaviours represents a different level of adult intervention than that examined in Chapter 2. To create interesting and varied opportunities for literacy requires some planning and some resourcing and, as we have seen, may even need teachers or other adults to become involved with the play. The word intervention is for some people somewhat suspect when used in association with young children's play; however, most adults already involve themselves in some form of initial planning when they think about setting up a themed play centre. Unlike areas that simply contain general collections of objects and in which the children can elect to play whatever they choose, a themed area implies a degree of intent on the part of the adult. The choice of theme can be influenced by many different factors: the formal curriculum, interests arising from the children, previous play centre themes, availability of resources, and the age and experience of the children. For our purposes an important additional factor is the extent to which literacy can be associated with the theme, and it is this which will form the substance of this section.

For experienced staff initial planning is often relatively easy, but for those with less experience who want to develop powerful literacy work with play, we will briefly explore some points worth thinking about. It is important to remember that all planning is a matter of exploring opportunities and making professional judgments, and that plans are not laws; professionals must always be prepared to modify plans if they do not work or if better ideas emerge.

A play setting can become literacy-enriched if you follow some of the suggestions listed below.

1. Choose a theme that naturally has a range of literacy activities associated with it.

   If the play is to have literacy as a natural element, then above all else the theme must be one in which literacy can occur in ways seen by the children as appropriate, relevant and interesting. While a truly creative mind could get literacy into anything, it is much easier with some themes than others. A medieval castle may be a brilliant setting in which to play, but this period was not one in which many people wrote and read. Turning the medieval castle into a modern visitor's attraction gets round this problem and introduces a wide range of literacy-related possibilities.

2. Choose a setting that is relevant to the children's lives but also has the capacity for extending and developing their knowledge.

   While children are usually willing to play at anything, literacy-related play is likely to be richer if they have some understanding of the theme. Children in different parts of the world and from different cultures will need themes relating to the lives. A farm might be relevant to young children in rural areas of the UK, but might be more puzzling in urban London. At the same time, the educational intention may well be to move beyond what they already know at the start, so while there need to be connections, there must also be possibilities for extending knowledge.

3. Visit a real example of your intended setting, if feasible.

   As we have just indicated, the natural use of literacy in play is likely to be increased if the children have some experience of the area chosen for the theme. Using visits to real settings can be a powerful way of extending and enhancing the repertoire of knowledge that children bring to playing. Visits can also be used to enhance the awareness of participants' roles, as well as of the context and the use of literacy. Be aware that the gender roles of people in the settings visited may not always as neutral as you would like. As a result of the visit the children will know much more about the who, when, why, where, what and how of literacy in the play setting. Advance discussion of topics can help focus the children's looking at particular elements, raising such questions as: where and when do you think people will be reading and writing, what signs and notices will you see, and who is doing the reading and writing? Also, do not forget that a visit can also be a literacy experience in its own right; children can take clipboards to record the important and interesting things they see.

4. Choose a setting that can have more than one distinct area.

Creating maximum opportunities for reading and writing can be aided by selecting a setting divisible into distinct areas. If a theme represents an area that has distinct parts then you increase the probable range of literacy experiences that might be associated with that area. Having chosen the overall theme for the centre, it is useful to consider if this offers the potential for areas of subdivision. It may also be the case that the various sub-areas offer differing literacy experiences which you would like the children to explore as the play continues.

One classroom observed had chosen to have a zoo as their play area. When planning this example, the teacher considered a number of possible sub-areas. She did not want too many but was looking for a small number of distinct possibilities that offered different opportunities for play and literacy-related play. Her planning involved creating a repertoire of possibilities from which she would later select those she felt were most appropriate for the children.

She came up with three possibilities: zoo park, animal care centre and customer care centre. The zoo park was the place in which cages and enclosures would be situated, the animal care centre was where food preparation and medical support would be based, and the customer care area would include a mixture of things such as offices, lost children, entrance booths, shop and cafe. Do remember that at this stage you are exploring the potential of the theme, and your explorations do not all need to be carried forward into practice. Even if there is very little space available, it is worth thinking about different areas at the planning stage, as this provides for a comprehensive perspective on the theme. Remember also that even a table with some appropriate bits and pieces might operate very effectively as an area. You do not necessarily need lots of space.

In fact, only two major areas were selected by this teacher who found it more appropriate to use small toy animals on a table top to represent the zoo park. This enabled the zoo park to exist as part of the play but take up very little space in the classroom. Children have no problem alternating between real-life-scale and small-scale toys.

5. Choose a setting that has a rich range of literate character roles.

You next need to consider the people associated with these areas. The point of doing this is that you can then explore the kinds of literacy that might be associated with these roles. Again, it is useful to think widely to explore fully the potential of the play centre. At this stage you may recognise that some characters may have more appeal than others and that some may seem to be more important. You need to be aware that while all children can play anyone, some will have very stereotyped views about who can be what. While some settings may appear to reinforce such stereotypical playing, with encouragement and discussion children can easily be persuaded to explore different roles.

When the teacher in our study explored the roles in each area of the zoo she came up with:

Zoo park	Animal care centre	Customer care centre
Animal keepers	Food preparers	Managers
Cleaners	Vets	Office workers
Customers	Cleaners	Ticket sales staff
Gardeners	Veterinary assistants	Customers
Security staff		Receptionists
Guides		Sales staff
		Cafeteria staff

It is clear that most, if not all of these people, would in their working lives be using literacy in some way.

6. Choose a setting in which people use different kinds of print for different purposes.

Thinking about personnel is really a starting point for considering the range of literacy-related activities involved in each role. Although this is a relatively simple listing activity, it never ceases to surprise us or the teachers we have worked with just how numerous and varied can be the results. In most cases literacy will be involved in both a professional and a personal sense. For example, a job sheet might be part of the professional literacy of a keeper, while a postcard from a colleague on holiday is part of their personal or social literacy. The exploration of these literacy activities will also help in the provision of the area. If children are going to play at some of these then they need the right materials to do so.

The teacher in the class we studied ended up with the following overall structure:

Zoo park	Animal care centre	Customer care centre
	Character roles	
Animal keepers	Food preparers	Managers
Cleaners	Vets	Office workers
Customers	Cleaners	Ticket sales staff
Gardeners	Veterinary assistants	Customers
Security staff		Receptionists
Guides		Sales staff
		Cafeteria staff
	Print items used in above roles	
Maps	Bills/receipts	Letters/memos
Signs	Record books	Calendars
Cage labels	Reference books	Job sheets
Descriptions of animals	Recipes	Tickets
Feeding instructions	Medical records	Guidebooks
Warning notices	Prescriptions	Notices/signs
Posters	Work rotas	Adverts
Rules	Wage slips	Books
Accident book	Forms	Activity sheets
Forms	Memos	Menus
Record sheets	Medicine labels	Cheques
Holiday chart	Order forms	Order forms

Figure 3.2: The complete zoo structure

Clearly, many things might be added to these lists and, in addition, there would be many more general items of environmental print. It can be helpful to add another layer to this chart – resources. This can ensure that the provision in the play centre is both comprehensive and appropriate. Clearly all the above items presume that appropriate resources are available. For instance, the office or the animal care centre might have a computer and it might be possible to find programmes or CD-roms that contain information about animals. It might be useful to have a typewriter, pre-printed forms and charts. It would be helpful if reference books were available so that children could make their own leaflets and guides for customers and staff.

7. Allow the children to design and build the setting.

   If the class or group have visited a related real setting, then they will already have ideas about what is needed as the setting is being built and developed. It is vital that children's views are taken into account and that they are allowed to develop some of the area. Interest and motivation will always be more intense if the children can appropriate the play area and feel that they own it. While it is always tempting to use commercial products to create a sense of authenticity, items built by children, however crude to adult eyes, will make the children feel closely involved with literacy. One classroom we observed had a kitchen as their play setting. Instead of using expensive commercial child-size replicas of kitchen appliances, every item was made by the five-year-old children using little more than large cardboard boxes. In this way they made fridges, freezers, microwaves, cookers, dishwashers and several other items. Apart from the development of craft skills, such building involved a lot of literacy. In order to make their models look right, children went home and examined their own family's kitchen appliances. They drew and copied, and sought, not only physically to build, but also to include all relevant literacy. So kitchen items included all the letters, words and numbers that can be found on real items.

Figure 3.3: The kitchen with child-built items

The children had observed the relevant environmental print and then used it to create more authentic items. Far from missing the neatness and precision of the commercially-produced play items (most of which do not contain the relevant print) the children played with a real sense of ownership. From the start, literacy was important in this setting and once a lot of other small kitchen-related print items had been added, the play was intense, frequently involved activities for which literacy was a critical part and gave children the sense of being literate people functioning in a print-rich world.

8. Occasionally, join the children and play in the setting.

Despite a visit, and despite discussion, almost any setting will have more potential than the children realise. Probably the best way to help them understand this is if you (or another adult) develop characters and become part of the play. In this way you can model ways of using literacy, help demonstrate purposes for literacy and reinforce the knowledge that the children are using. Do include some of the strategies outlined at the end of Chapter 2. Looking at video of some literacy-related play could be part of the children's literacy education. Do take some time to discuss with the class what you have seen going on in the play and draw children's attention to interesting examples of literacy products that result from the play; these can be powerful models for other children.

CHAPTER 4

Play, literacy and events

In this chapter we want to explore in more detail why play and literacy work so well together and to consider how the relationships we have examined so far can be extended.

We know that play is a highly motivating experience for young children. It has a sense of authenticity and attracts a degree of commitment unmatched by most other school experiences. In play, children involve themselves with aspects of life that often demand that they think and behave like people acting upon the world outside school. The 'real world' is a very complex place and engaging with that world demands involvement in a rich variety of experiences. Handling the 'real' world in play demands a degree of reality within the play itself and yet the 'real' in play has a flexible relationship with the 'unreal'. As Heath (1983: 164–5) pointed out:

> The constraints of reality enter into the play which accompanies these socio-dramas in yet other ways. Once the children have announced a suspension of reality by declaring a sandbox a city, a rock, a little girl, or a playroom corner a kitchen, they paradoxically more often than not insist on a strict adherence to certain details of real-life behaviour. In playing with doll babies, girls insist they are not dressed unless a diaper is pinned about them. Children in a play kitchen will break their routine of washing dishes by reaching over to stir the contents of a pot on the stove. When asked why they do this, they reply 'Hit'll burn.'

This coexistence of the real and pretend is the key to offering children deeper experiences, which link their world of play to the wider world outside school and infancy.

The nature of literacy

The key to exploring this relationship at a deeper level is to consider the way literacy has been redefined in recent years. Historically, reading and writing were perceived as relatively straightforward. All you had to do was learn a set of combinations of sounds and letters and, hey presto, you were a reader (and, with some handwriting practice, a writer). During the twentieth century the relationship between literacy and people became more complex and in the last quarter literacy was rediscovered as a social phenomenon. Of course 'rediscovered' is a misleading word as literacy itself has never been anything other than a social phenomenon. People have always used literacy in social contexts. While technical knowledge of phonics may be a necessary component of being literate in the twenty-first century Western world, on its own it provides a very partial notion of what it means to be a literate person.

Conventionally, school has been the institution through which children were inducted into knowledge of reading and writing. If all the articles, books, pamphlets and pieces on literacy were piled up, most of them would be seen to be associated with learning to be a reader and writer in school. Literacy is probably the most exhaustively studied curriculum area and, as every reader of newspapers can attest, it is still the curriculum area that features most predominantly in people's minds. However, alongside the continuing, seemingly inexhaustible studies of classroom literacy has been developing a range of studies from historians, anthropologists, sociologists and semioticians which have started to position literacy rather differently from how it is normally conceived within schooling. It is a view that is often at odds with the conventional school notions of literacy, and when the two perspectives are examined, it is schooling which is left having to answer the biggest questions. As Barton (1991:3) pointed out, 'Most theories of literacy start out from the educational settings in which literacy is typically taught. These views of what literacy is are often at odds with what people experience in their everyday lives.' Perhaps the easiest way of illustrating this is to do something that for a century literacy researchers failed to do, and that is consider how people actually use literacy in their lives.

Literacy in everyday life

What characterises the experience and use of literacy beyond and outside school? A growing body of research (including, Heath 1983; Fishman 1988; Street 1995; Barton 1994; Voss 1996; Finders 1997; and Barton and Hamilton 1998) suggests a number of important qualities of everyday literacy life.

1. Literacy is almost always highly meaningful to people's lives and often results from personal choices.

   While people may not always like using literacy, it is well understood as having significance in everyday life. Print in myriad forms impacts upon people in a multitude of ways and much of it is intimately associated with personal lifestyle choices; hobbies, interests, work, sport, etc. all bring literacy into people's lives.

2. Literacy is both initiated and responded to by users.

   In everyday life literacy is often imposed upon people. Sometimes we have to fill in forms, respond to bills and follow instructions. But equally as frequently we initiate activities that draw in literacy. We write to people, we request information, we read our newspapers and so on. We opt to engage in the use of literacy because it enables us to achieve things in our lives that are of personal importance and significance.

3. Literacy is used to make things happen – it is a means to an end, embedded in wider events, and success is measured by whether it achieves these ends.

In our everyday lives we tend not to use literacy for its own sake. It is almost always used in the pursuit of some other end. We don't make lists to practise list making; we make lists because they have a function for us. That function is part of a much more powerful event, perhaps ensuring the family has food. The list plays a part in achieving this; it is not an end in itself. Success is not measured by how neatly the list is written or whether it is correctly spelled, but by whether the appropriate items end up on the table.

4. Literacy is located in a social past and future; it comes out of prior experience and connects to future experience.

Many of people's literacy-related encounters are related to and derived from past events and experiences. Equally many will have a relationship to people's futures. Because literacy is so deeply embedded in people's lives it is often the means by which past, present and future in personal and social lives are connected. It is part of the way we make sense of ourselves as human beings.

5. Literacy is used for a very wide range of purposes, involves a wide range of sources and audiences, and varies in the demands it makes upon users.

It would be very hard to keep a complete record of all the reading and writing experiences encountered, all the sources used and audiences involved in an average week. Everyday we engage in multiple engagements with many different kinds of print. Some are easy for us (making a note for milkman) while the others might be very hard (understanding a tax form). Our relationship with literacy is continuously moving through these different dimensions.

6. Literacy is often highly social.

While some literacy experiences often appear individual, they are nevertheless rooted in social experiences as the relationship with the source or audience changes. Often the social nature is more explicitly revealed, as in newspaper reading when one person says to another, 'Did you see this bit about . . . ?' Varenne and McDermott (1986) recorded an example where a mother was unsure whether the ointment in the medicine cabinet was appropriate for her baby's eye problem. Her husband also read the instructions and then the elder daughter, and as the mother was still unsure, she ended up phoning the pharmacist and reading the instructions to him. Barton and Padmore (1991) pointed out that many of us, when unsure about something we are reading or writing, consult friends or neighbours, or even approach consultants such as accountants or specialists on computer helplines. Engaging with print often means engaging with other people.

7. Literacy is often a highly enjoyable experience, is sometimes challenging, and sometimes defeats everyone.

Using literacy can be a real burden as the demands are sometimes very complex. (This is why so much money is spent employing people with specialist knowledge: lawyers, accountants and other professionals not only know their subject but can read and write the languages involved in them.) However, literacy can result in very satisfying and enjoyable experiences. The existence of bookshops, newsagents and the internet are testimony to the fact that literacy enables human beings to meet many different kinds of needs and to enjoy doing so.

8. Literacy is used in different ways by different communities who have different values for and beliefs about literacy.

Street (1984) uses the term 'ideological literacy' to characterise the ways in which literacy occurs in daily life. By ideological literacy is meant types of literacy which draw their meanings and use from being situated within cultural values and practices. Because cultures differ in the things they value and practise, literacy will differ both at a deep level and at a surface level. An ideological model of literacy suggests that there are literacies rather than literacy and that the use of these literacies creates engagement, involves wider networks, and is consistently related to the everyday lives of people in their communities.

Literacy in schools

Is the out-of-school richness, variety and flexibility of literacy use matched by literacy life in classrooms? On the whole the answer seems to be, 'no.' Literacy in schools has a quite different character:

1. Literacy is almost always imposed upon children, forcing them to be responders and seldom initiators.

Children's literacy experience is predetermined by many people other than themselves. In the case of the UK, it is by the author of the *Framework for Teaching* documentation that guides almost every child's school literacy life. Their literacy lives are always in response mode – they answer questions, write about teacher-selected topics, fill in worksheets and work books. They mostly do only what school tells them to do. It is rare that they are able to initiate the use of literacy.

2. Literacy is seldom meaningful and relevant to children's lives as people.

From a child's perspective the school's literacy choices are arbitrary and do not relate to their own concerns and interests. They are not intrinsically meaningful to children. If they become meaningful, then it is probably as a means to distorted ends – for praise, for stars, for tests success, or at some distant and almost unimaginable point in the future, getting a job. It is noticeable that despite young children's out-of-school lives being so related to popular culture, this is almost completely excluded from the literacy curriculum in schools (Marsh and Millard 2000). As Street and Street (1991: 143) put it, 'Non-school literacies have come to be seen as inferior attempts at the real thing, to be compensated for by enhanced schooling'.

3. Literacy is seldom used to make things happen in the world; exercises are treated as ends in themselves – as here and now activities – and success is measured by performance on the task.

Administrative convenience ensures that almost all school literacy tasks are exercises, and it is getting the exercise done that forms the purpose for the activity. Success with literacy is about correctness in the exercise, not about the use of literacy having achieved something purposeful and worthwhile beyond its own execution. Literacy in schooling is not situated within more complex social events; it is separated from its relationship to the real world.

4. Literacy is usually experienced through exercises with a narrow focus; it involves a limited range of specially privileged purposes and audiences, and makes relatively constant demands upon users.

Exercises always alter the nature of literacy. They have to in order that the activity can last fifteen minutes or fit a page in a workbook. Literacy gets sliced up into manageable fragments rather than existing as a coherent experience. Levels of difficulty are always carefully managed and the audience is almost always the teacher wearing an assessor's hat. Schools assign differing status to different aspects of literacy, meaning that only certain kinds of texts get read or written, regardless of how motivating and meaningful the excluded texts are to children. This results in one of the paradoxes of schooling in that the kinds of texts most privileged in schools are the ones least likely to be pursued once people leave schooling. Most adults do not write stories, poems, or essays in their everyday lives (Hall 1989).

5. Literacy has only a past and future in relation to difficulty; in other words, connections across literacy practices are not related to previous or future meanings or uses but simply to being easier or more difficult.

   School is a bizarre experience. Usually children arrive in the morning, get told what to do, they do it and go home. It starts all over again the next day, and so on. Thus, literacy does not connect to a social past or social future; so much of the literacy in school has no function beyond its use as an exercise and it is difficult to build it into a meaningful time continuum. For children the future is doing more workbook pages or writing more pages in their exercise books. The future is harder work, not more meaningful experiences of literacy.

6. Literacy is usually experienced as individual practice.

   With its focus on individual development, much of literacy use in schools is also, in practical terms, individual. Children do their own exercises on their own worksheets, answer questions individually and have their work marked individually. Children are often put in a competitive position in classrooms, as cooperation and sharing mitigate against the individualised structure of learning, as well as being noisier and generating products that are more difficult to mark.

7. Literacy is defined in narrow and decontextualised ways, which govern interpretations, choices and modes of practice, and assessment.

   Street (1984) refers to these kinds of practices as representing an 'autonomous' model of literacy. By autonomous literacy is meant a model of literacy in which literacy is separated from the wider social world of its actual use, and is treated as a neutral object to be studied, analysed and mastered as a technical skill. In schools literacy is treated as an autonomous phenomenon; one that has a life-world of its own, unconnected to the ways in which it is actually used by people in their lives. Wagner (1993), after studying schooling and literacy in Morocco, wrote, 'Literacy skills taught in school may bear only a partial resemblance to the kinds of abilities and knowledge utilised in the performance of literacy tasks in everyday life'. (p.188). It is no different anywhere else.

Comparing the literacy models

Juliebo (1985) vividly highlighted the contrasts between these two models of literacy (although not naming them as ideological and autonomous) when she compared the literacy experiences of very young children at home with their experiences in kindergarten. She commented (p.132–3):

- In the home the child was the main initiator of literacy learning whereas in school the teacher was the initiator and the children's attempts to initiate were not accessed.
- At home, sharing and reciprocity were constantly manifest. In the kindergarten, in general, the children had to reciprocate in the predetermined programme, the construction of which was not mutually shared between the teacher and learner.
- Many activities in kindergarten were only concerned with the here and now and precluded transcendence. This was particularly true of work time and art activities. At home transcendence was present in most children's literacy interactions.
- At school, literacy activities were not grounded in the children's own life worlds, and as a result often lacked meaning. This was in strong contrast to the home where literacy was a part of everyday life. Interactions in the home were almost always accompanied by a joyful sharing.

If this level of contrast exists for children in the usually less formal world of kindergarten and nursery then it must be much greater as children move on up the school. Yet, the almost tragic irony is that the primary justification for teaching literacy in school is to enable people to use it successfully in the complex social world outside school.

The gulf between in-school and out-of-school in the way literacy is treated and used seems considerable. However, it must be appreciated that schools cannot be the same as homes. Historically, schools have always faced the problem of teaching large numbers of children and doing so in ways that are efficient and economically viable. The result is a system that has developed particular administrative, social and curriculum structures to enable this to happen and it is difficult to see how the essential nature of such structures is going to change in the near future, if ever. The price that is paid is the separation of the school curriculum from the real world, and this applies to literacy in particular. The major problem with reducing this drift towards separation is that the autonomous use of literacy is so firmly institutionalised within and beyond schooling, and is currently being reinforced so strongly by recent political moves in many countries (the adoption of the National Curriculum in the UK, and the creation of state-wide curriculums in both the US and Australia) that major structural change is unlikely. Does this mean that it is impossible to present young children with a more realistic experience of literacy, or is there a place within conventional schooling where this can be achieved?

The interrelationship between play and literacy

What might it mean for a school to create situations which reflected ideological as well as autonomous literacy practices?

- What if sometimes the children were not distanced from real-world purposes for literacy, if language was not distanced by being used solely for analytic purposes, and if literacy experiences derived from a complex social situation rather than from the ritualistic performance demands of school literacy tasks?
- What if sometimes narratives were not privileged and the genres used derived from the social need, if texts were problematic and raised issues that confronted children's beliefs about the world and their roles and rights, and if children were treated as knowers and doers rather than as ignorant and passive?
- What if sometimes the children's work was not assessed, if situations explored transcended the artificial barriers of school and classroom walls, and if children were not even conscious that they were learning about literacy?
- What if sometimes children could really care about situations and felt they could act towards them in a literate way?

We believe that in early years education the response to the above questions has to be a positive one, and the mechanism for achieving this is the relationship between literacy and socio-dramatic play. What is it about socio-dramatic play and how children use it in school that makes it so appropriate for this task? Very simply, as the evidence of chapters 2 and 3 makes clear, it shares many of the underlying characteristics of ideological literacy.

Socio-dramatic play is fully meaningful and enjoyable to children and is usually initiated by them. It often draws on children's real-world experiences and knowledge. The meanings of play are not historically and politically determined by the institutions of schooling but relate to concerns of the lives of people as lived outside schooling. As Paley (1988: 6) said, 'Images of good and evil, birth and death, parent and child, move in and out of the real and the pretend. There is no small talk. The listener is submerged in philosophical position papers, a virtual recapitulation of life's enigmas.'

Within socio-dramatic play a huge range of topics occur, and those topics draw on a wide range of sources and involve a range of roles. The demand upon players is not a constant but will vary according to role, situation and event.

In this type of play, children initiate events and as co-players respond to other people's initiations. Play is often structured in events, thus the elements of the play are grounded in the events; these elements are not played for their own sake – they are means to ends. Within these events, the action is coherent and the success of play is not measured by performance in the elements but by the satisfaction of the players about the whole event.

Many aspects of play within events can be related to literacy, and this literacy is a means to an end: not experienced for its own sake. Play is not assessed and children are free to explore what it means to be an active, knowing, literate human being rather than continue to fit the conventional school role that positions them only as immature learners.

Thus children's play, like everyday literacy practices, draws meaning from being situated within cultural histories, values and practices and thus generates engagement, involves networks and is consistently related to the everyday lives of people in their communities. In socio-dramatic play literacy often has a pivotal role. It could been seen as a lubricant which eases social interaction. It is a device for engaging in many kinds of relationship; it can start relationships, it can end relationships; it ranges across a whole host of human obligations and freedoms, eases explanations, conveys knowledge and imposes burdens and constraints.

When literacy occurs within play, as evidenced in Chapter 3, it appears in contexts which require use of literacy to fulfil many functions. The order at the chippy or the letters to the cook arose out of the context created by the play. However, almost inevitably, such responses will mostly be restricted to situations within the knowledge and experience of children. In this chapter we want to consider how teachers might use the attraction and intensity of play as a way of extending children's understanding of: the context of the setting; the purposes for writing; and the forms of text, which might otherwise not occur naturally within their play.

This sounds both interventionist and manipulative. To a degree it is, just as is all teaching which puts an external demand on children. However, in this case, the intervention is not necessarily directly within the play itself beyond, maybe, identifying areas for play and ensuring that they are built up and developed. Thus, we are not suggesting much beyond what many teachers do already in facilitating socio-dramatic play experiences. Nor are we suggesting that what children do when they play within the area should be controlled or directed by the teacher. We are very happy for a play area to be used by children to play in whatever way they want. In a themed area the play will often relate to the theme, but not always. Play is a fluid activity and a scene in a hospital can transform into a domestic scene in an almost seamless way.

What we are suggesting is that teachers use the interest in and motivation of children towards socio-dramatic play to provide literacy experiences that relate to the theme, and provide wider experience of issues relating to the theme. In recent years teachers have become increasingly aware of the need to ensure that even the youngest children have access to a wide range of text forms. It is not sufficient (important though they are) to restrict children to stories and news. In England, the National Curriculum and the Literacy Strategy make specific demands that children experience what is called 'non-chronological writing', and in the US the guidelines of the IRA/NCTE Standards Project also had a specific comment that 'Students understand and control a range of genres and purposes'. Both the National Curriculum and the Standards Project emphasise the importance of writing for different audiences.

Of course, teachers can provide direct experiences of writing in different genres (or text forms) through exercises and demonstrations. But as linguists make clear, genres developed out of social contexts; they evolved and continue to evolve in response to social need. The experience of learning about a way of writing is much more significant and relevant when the demand seems necessary and relevant to the learner. Socio-dramatic play can make the experience of using and understanding genres much easier. When children are committed to their play then writing in response to demands that link closely to that play generates a strong sense of authenticity about purposes for writing.

The notion of events

Most teachers have no problems in thinking of themes for play areas. If they do, then children will have no hesitation in offering ideas. It is difficult to think of any areas which cannot have writing related to them in some ways, although it will clearly be easier in some than in others. In the course of our work during the last two years we have seen many different areas in action. In classes of four-year-olds we have seen the Three Bears' cottage, an estate agency, a restaurant, and local library. In classes of five-year-olds we have seen a castle, a fire station, a building site, a dentist, a canal boat, a cave, a gift shop and, as you will see soon, a garage. In classes of six-year-olds we have seen a modern kitchen, an old-fashioned kitchen, a local library, an old-fashioned laundry, and a toy store. In classes of seven-year-olds we have seen recently the channel tunnel, a school office, travel agents, and a veterinary surgery. In classes of much older children we have seen an environmental centre, a space centre, a television studio and a railway station. Alongside all these play areas occurred experiences within which print had a major role.

Within each of these play areas the children played in the same kinds of ways as were indicated in Chapter 2. However, alongside the play in the play areas, the children experienced events related to the play. Few who were there will forget when a message arrived in the classroom about a pet stuck up a tree, how the fire crew responded with alacrity. The five-year-old fire person rescuing the cat from the tree carefully ascended the ladder, delicately reached up for the (toy) cat, grabbed it by its tail and flung it to the floor. The news reporters who were watching made great use of this when afterwards they wrote about the rescue.

Many of the play areas mentioned above offered opportunities for events to occur outside the play itself. In all these related events, writing or reading was involved. In some there was a great deal, in some it was relatively little and in some there was no writing at all. These accompanying events were not 'literacy' events. They were events which involve people in solving problems (rescuing the cat), getting on with their work, and exploring issues and ideas. Literacy occurs within these events (the writing of the newspaper report) just as it does in events outside and beyond school. It is because these events occur in response to different needs, because they involve different people, and because they have different relationships with society, that the nature of the writing involved covers a wide spectrum of text forms.

Thus a central feature of the move for greater coherence of literacy within socio-dramatic play is the notion of events. As we have indicated above, it is the the structure of an event that gives meaning and purpose to literacy. In order to see more clearly why events are an important construct for literacy in play, we need to unpack the idea by exploring one in more detail, and we will take a common, typical everyday event: going shopping for food.

An event usually starts with a meaning and this can be characterised in a relatively straightforward way. A food shopping event could be characterised as getting food to feed the self or family. This meaning is really a purpose and this purpose creates the context within which a lot of elements of this event have a place and function.

Where does a food shopping event start? It could start in many places: feeling hungry, realising there is not sufficient food in the kitchen, and so on. How does it proceed? There may be a recipe consulted or there may be a list made. There may be a visit to the supermarket that involves driving past road signs and directions. It may involve walking round the supermarket using the list, reading prices or other information, selecting the items and placing them in the basket. It may involve paying with a credit card, checking the receipt, going back home and putting food away. All very straightforward.

However, certain points need to made.

- It is clear that literacy is either embedded or has the potential to be embedded in this event and can occur at a number of points in it. The events also can involve both writing and reading. Some of the literacy might be very simple, while other parts might be quite complex.
- Any literacy is given purpose by the event. Lists are not written for the sake of writing, nor are packets read to practice reading. The event creates a context for the literacy and gives it meaning. Literacy becomes a means to an end, not the end itself. The packet is read for information, not for practice.
- Literacy is not the only feature of this event. It shares a place with many other elements. These could be construed as a variety of curriculum areas. There might be *economic* decisions about how the overall family budget might be affected by the purchasing during the event. There might be *mathematical* decisions in counting the cost of the purchases or comparing the value of different products or special offers. There might be *health* decisions as cans and packets are read for dietary information. There might be *political* and *ethical* decisions about whether to purchase food from certain countries. There might be *biological* decisions about whether to buy something that has been genetically modified. The point is that in real life events, literacy exists alongside many other elements that are part of achieving the same purpose. Literacy is not isolated from its association with other elements.
- Problems might occur. The supermarket might be out of stock of a favourite item so suddenly new information has be sought, items compared and prices checked. Problems force action, in this case more precise reading and greater use of mathematics.

It is, of course, possible that any of the elements of this event could be pulled out and practised as a curriculum event in schooling. It is almost certainly important to do this, so that particular skills can be developed and practised. But to experience only the deconstructed elements of this event is to miss the way they all hang together in a coherent real life experience.

It is this complexity that needs to be sought in the play area.

Using events in or in association with socio-dramatic play

At the end of chapter three, we chose the example of a zoo-based socio-dramatic play area and considered how such a setting might be developed to include a range of literacy-related materials. So far we have considered who works in the zoo and what kinds of literacy are associated with their occupations. We would like to extend this example and consider how, within this setting, events might be developed to provide experiences that extend and challenge children's knowledge of literacy and allow them to act as literate people.

We can imagine an area of the classroom that contains perhaps two of the areas we identified earlier: an administrative area and some actual cages in an animal house. There will be a number of large signs with the name of the zoo and prices for admission. The administrative area will have all the features of a typical office with a section having a booth so that tickets can be bought by visitors. The other area might have a series of boxes made to look like cages, each of which has a label on the outside and toy animals inside. A couple of these could be the more ferocious animals.

We are now looking for events that have some complexity, can utilise a range of literacy experiences, include other areas of world knowledge and create a degree of problematicity for the children. The diagram below makes a number of suggestions. This is hardly a complete list of possible events, but it is nevertheless a range of quite interesting ones with many possibilities.

The first consideration always has to be how to introduce an event. It might need something in the area to change or it might be as a result of outside intervention. Whichever it is, it can make a real difference if the event begins in a dramatic way. For instance, if the area has been set up and the children arrive one morning to find the lion's cage door open and the lion gone. The authenticity of the event might be aided by some straw scattered across the classroom and even a muddy paw print or two. A really clever teacher might even arrange for a recording of a lion roaring to be played just outside the classroom door, and some urgent notes to arrive in from other teachers saying how they have heard the lion roaring and how all their children are frightened (and notes could also come from children in other classes). The notes could ask if the lion has escaped and if so, what are they going to do about it.

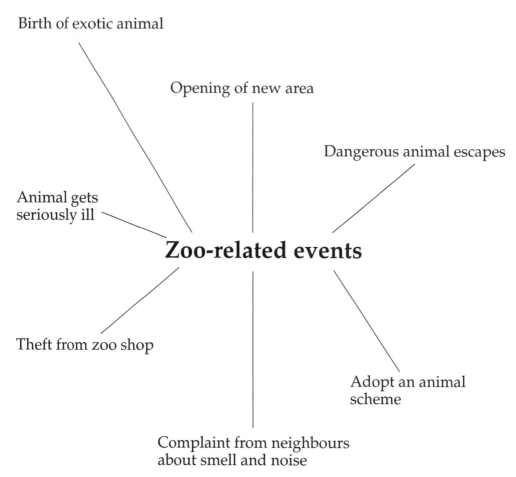

Figure 4.1: Zoo-related events

A whole range of responses are possible. The first has to be discussion and the adults would be well-advised to have a tape-recorder running during this discussion. In our experience quite wonderful discussions occur when there is a real sense of drama.

The children could go round the school asking if anyone has seen their lion. The children could respond in writing to reassure the children in the other classes. The children could write a press release about it. They could do wanted posters with a description and drawings of the animal. They could create instructions for what to do if the lion is seen. There could be an inspection to try and ascertain how the lion escaped and a health and safety report could be written. A set of instructions about new safety procedures could be created. Some of these activities might involve other curriculum areas, so the children might not only read about lions but also draw and paint them, design an escape-proof cage and discuss the ethics of keeping wild animals in cages.

We are not suggesting that all these are done. As in Chapter 3, we are only suggesting possibilities. Professionals can make their choices about what might be appropriate for their children. There might be some readers who are thinking, 'How on earth could young children do some of these things, especially if they do not know much about writing?' The answer to this question demands reading Chapter 5 in this book, when writing a letter of reassurance starts to look too easy for five-year-olds.

Some practical points

In the UK the ways of using play and events may have to vary according to the setting. Settings operating fully within the *Curriculum Guidance for the Foundation Stage* have great freedom. Those operating within the *Framework for Teaching* and the *Literacy Hour* may have much less. For the second group all is not lost, and to a large extent the full contextualisation of literacy that goes on in event-based play and literacy more than justifies the inclusion of play within the literacy curriculum. However, the way it operates may have to change.

If the event is introduced by a literacy object, for instance a letter arriving in the zoo that complains about the noise of animals at night, then the letter can very easily become the centre of the text-based teaching element of the literacy hour. A clever teacher might make sure that this letter has certain textual features within it that fit a particular literacy hour topic. Thus, the letter can be read, re-read, examined, analysed, and reflected upon in the same way as any text that features in such a lesson. It might also be the case that during the twenty-minutes group work, one group could go into the Zoo area and write their responses, enabling some of the work to occur within the area. This, of course, is not the playing and it is still necessary for groups of children to actually play at being in the zoo. It is the playing that creates the interest, motivation, engagement and context, such that the events, when they occur, are sufficiently meaningful to capture the children's interest.

It is also possible that some literacy events could have associated activities built into some of the playing. For instance, if the scenario outlined in the previous section (the escaping animals) was introduced, then materials could be provided in the play area such that children could incorporate responses into their play as in Chapter 2.

At the time of writing, there does seem to be an increasing relaxation of the utter formality of the teaching of literacy that existed when the framework was first introduced, and in recent months we have seen more and more classroom teachers feeling able to build playing into the curriculum. Perhaps the time is right for more teachers to explore the richness of literacy response that can arise when linking play and literacy. In the next chapter many of these ideas are examined within a detailed case study.

CHAPTER 5

A case study: the garage

Background

In this chapter we are going to describe the writing that was experienced by a class of children in association with a socio-dramatic play area. Our intention is not to tell teachers how to set up and carry out such play, but to document the ways in which writing featured as part of the overall experience associated with the play. We have set out to write this chapter as a narrative of what happened, but inevitably our account can give no more than a few insights into the richness of experiences and behaviour of the children. To facilitate our 'telling' we have divided our story into a number of sections. These sections contain episodes that did not always occur in chronological order; they are, however, gathered into episodes to maintain coherence and to ensure that related events are kept together.

The children were aged between 4.5 years and 5.5 years. Some of them had just started school and others had started later in the previous school year. They were what is described as a mixed-age class, being partly reception children (the year of entry to school) and partly year one children (the second year in school). The range of experience and level of skill in writing was, as a consequence, quite varied but it was thought to be important that all children had access to the writing being done in association with play. The school was in an urban setting and the building was old, having been built in the 1890s. The classroom was quite small and the teacher had to use the limited space imaginatively. As is often the case, the play area was situated in a corner of the classroom, next to a variety of activity tables.

It was the teacher's decision that the socio-dramatic play area would be a garage. This was because the school had a policy that all the socio-dramatic areas would be related and the theme for that term was 'transport'. The 'Garage' experience began at the beginning of the term in January and ran through to the beginning of April.

Writing and play were already powerful experiences in the lives of these children. They had been encouraged to write independently from starting school. They were encouraged to try to spell words as they thought they heard them until such time as they showed signs of moving towards an awareness that there was more to spelling than sounds. In both their reading and in the context of their own writing they would discuss phonics, but this was not over emphasised. They were encouraged to consider themselves as authors and generally had every confidence in their writing ability. The writing activities usually took place within the context of an integrated day where a number of different curriculum activities were being carried out in the classroom at the same time. To some extent these children used writing not to complete instructional activities but because it was a way of completing things they wanted to do. There was a considerable emphasis on using writing for personal and authentic reasons and, as a consequence, none of the children were afraid of writing and all wrote willingly.

Getting started: making a visit

A play area already existed in the classroom left over from the previous term. This had been a house. The first activity was a discussion of the closure of the house and the introduction of the idea of the garage. The teacher's role in the discussion was to interest and enthuse the children about the new area and her suggestion that the class could visit a real garage was greeted with excitement.

One important aspect of the teacher's preparation was to try and ensure that the children had some understanding about the business the play area represented. To some extent, probably all the children knew something about garages. However, their experience was much more likely to be of being in a car while petrol was bought than of the repairing and mending of cars. The initial discussion would be important in helping the children become aware of the wider and more varied functions. They did not need to know everything, as the play in the area would help to develop their awareness, but some initial information was felt to be useful.

A visit to a local garage, owned by Mr Pipe, was organised. Mr Pipe's garage was a small back-street garage and was purely concerned with the maintenance and repair of vehicles. Assistance was sought from willing helpers and a suitable date and time agreed with the garage owner. Just before the trip took place there was a discussion about what the children might look for, a few notes were made on a jotting sheet and several children were given clip boards on which to make notes of things they saw. The visit was used to draw attention to all kinds of environmental print, both outside and inside the garage. The physical setting was experienced and many objects examined and named for the children. The ramp or car-lift made a great impression. The various tools were examined and the children particularly noted that everything had its own special place to be returned to, something that they were to replicate in their own garage later. They took note of the cleaning of cars with the hose pipe, the changing of wheels and the use of oil. One particular feature, which impressed them greatly, was the noise, partly due to the mechanical activity but also because the mechanics worked with a radio blaring out. Both the garage workshop and the office were explored and items of equipment noted, including the 'pin-up' calendar on the office notice board. It is not always easy to explain political correctness to children and keep your host happy at the same time!

On return to the classroom there was a whole class discussion about what had been seen. They remembered things they had looked at and that Mr Pipe had talked about. As the discussion continued, the teacher made notes on the jotter sheet. This was to be referred to when the children progressed to other activities later.

The discussion provided the opportunity to talk about the kind of jobs being done and the roles which would later be part of the play in the garage play area. It also gave the chance to examine some of the items the garage owner had given them to take back to school: a fan belt, some spark plugs, some jump leads and switches. These were talked about and a range of things that can happen in garages were discussed. All this helped consolidate the experience of the visit and reinforced a technical vocabulary appropriate to garage-related concepts.

At the end of the discussion the teacher suggested that the children might like to write a thank you letter to Mr Pipe (see Examples 5.1 and 5.2). These letters reflected the discussion which had taken place as the children worked on their letters in groups. The teacher asked each group if they knew how to start a letter. Most children in the group seemed to know that 'Dear Mr Pipe' would be appropriate. The teacher showed the children how to set out their letter by writing 'Dear Mr Pipe' in the conventional place. Through further discussion, various ways of saying 'thank you' were considered. Each child was then encouraged to think of something special that they had noticed and liked about the garage. The letters, therefore, include some general kind of thank you and a more personal response. While the children wrote they were given lots of encouragement but also reminded to reread what they had written. The letters were then sent to the garage as they were, unedited and uncorrected.

Because the children's writing was valued as it was, and because the teachers (and the school) did not want children to think that writing was little more than correcting and writing neatly, it was usually the case that the writing was left as it was done. The teacher used the writing to inform herself about each child's knowledge of written language and then planned experiences accordingly. When contacting outside agencies and the general public, teachers need to consider their stance on using children's writing as it stands. Some teachers will have no doubts that the children's work is fine as it is. Others may feel that at least some translation is called for and, sometimes, editing and correction may be thought necessary. In this case the garage owner knew that the letters would be coming uncorrected and accepted them for what they were. All the children wrote 'thank you' letters but as a rule not every child did every piece of writing. It was thought sufficient that a writing activity was shared in some way with the class and over a period of time each child would gain a range of writing experiences which would be similar but not identical to every other child.

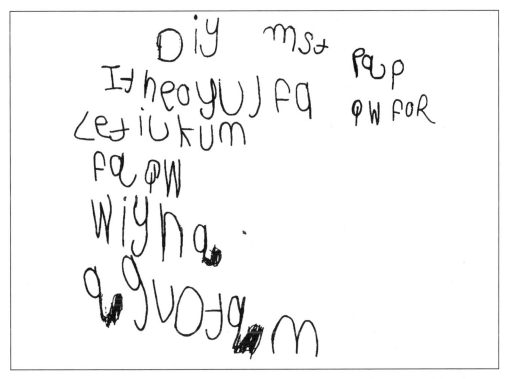

Example 5.1: Thank you letter to Mr Pipe. (*Dear Mr Pipe, I thank you for letting us come. Thank you. We had a good time*)

dear mr Pap

facw fur Letn vs cum to
your gorj I Lovd the Bumpybit
wiv the wot car

Example 5.2: Thank you letter to Mr Pipe. (*Dear Mr Pipe, Thank you for letting us come to your garage. I loved the bumpy bit with the white car.*)

Most play areas start fairly quickly after such a visit. In this case, because the children were going to build the area and everything in it, the moment at which the children would begin to play in it was a little way off. To fill this space and to help the children understand some rather fundamental points about how the real world worked, the teacher introduced some rather different experiences.

Event 1: Getting permission

As the children were excitedly planning and even beginning to build things for their play area, the teacher stopped the children and said that she had suddenly remembered that people could not simply build anything whenever or wherever they wanted: they had to have permission. At first the children wanted to rush to the headteacher for this 'permission', but the teacher then explained that permission had to come from the Town Hall Planning Department. The class discussed what they needed to ask and several of them wrote letters (see Examples 5.3 and 5.4). The teacher had previously arranged with someone at the Planning Department for a response to be sent.

This personal contact was important and agreement was easily obtained (indeed the people at the planning department were very pleased to help) and it created a considerable sense of authenticity for the children.

From phrases such as, 'to the Town Hall' and, 'can we have some planning permission' it is clear that the children have only a vague idea of what is involved here. But, which of us has not pondered over how to address the faceless, nameless body in official correspondence? For some of the children permission is in the same order of things as asking for a spanner or a ladder. This did not deter the teacher; as long as most things were within the children's understanding she felt that some new and difficult concepts could be tolerated. Indeed, such experiences were one of the ways in which they would learn that life was rather more complex than they had previously thought. This balance between the familiar and the novel experience is something with which teachers have to constantly juggle; getting the balance right is part of the skill of teaching.

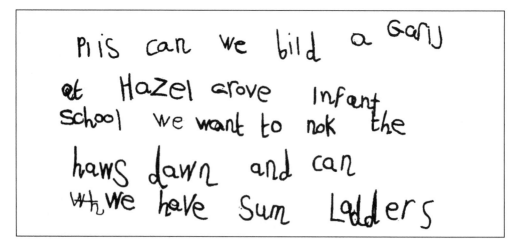

Example 5.3: Letter to Planning Department. (*Please can we build a garage at Hazel Grove Infant School We want to knock the house down and can we have some ladders*)

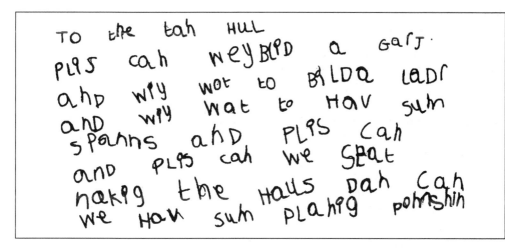

Example 5.4: Letter to Planning Department. (*To the Town Hall, Please can we build a garage and we want to build a ladder and we want to have some spanners and please can and please can we start knocking the house down Can we have some planning permission*)

The response from the Town Hall was to send an application form. Well, it is useful to get used to form filling as soon as possible! On one level, the form was quite a complex affair and the children needed a lot of help in reading what was on the form. However, most of the questions on the form were readily comprehended by the children. Questions about where, how big, dangerous substances, etc. made sense to them. With some help and discussion about what was being asked for, some of the more able writers were eager to have a go at providing the information required (see Example 5.5).

Apart from making amusing reading, with the size being quoted as '12 footsteps long and 9 wide' and the walls being made of corrugated card, form filling can serve a useful purpose. Forms invariably call for the writing of names and addresses, which are among the first important things we want our children to learn. Often a child who can write nothing else unaided can write their name. Form filling within play provides a functional and meaningful activity which requires only the minimum of skill and does not take too long – an added bonus for the beginner writer.

Drawing plans and getting ready

While some children were filling in planning forms, others were drawing plans for the garage and office (see Example 5.6). These also gave rise to discussion about what had been seen on the visit and what was needed in terms of resources. Labelling the items is a relatively easy writing task for the less confident children. The application form and plans were sent back to the Town Hall and the reply was awaited while other preparation continued.

PART ONE

Planning
Application Form

Please read the guidance notes which
will help you to complete this form.
4 copies of the form and 4 sets of
plans should be submitted.

1

Name and Address of Applicant and Agent

Name and Address of Applicant

Name Clare

Address Hazel grove
Chapul street
Hazel grove
Stockpot

Postcode SK74LB Daytime Tel. No. 483 431

Name and Address of Agent (if any)

Name

Address InFant school

Postcode   Daytime Tel. No.

Person to contact

2

Proposed Development

A Location or Address of Proposed Development

Hazel grove inFant school

B Description of Proposed Development (specify the number of units in the case of housing development)

Garage

12 Fust eps Long   9 Wad

C Size of Site (edge in red on submitted site plan)   hectare

D Is the proposal for a temporary period? Answer YES or NO [Yes] If yes, for how long un tol easter

E Do you own or control any adjoining land? (edge in blue on submitted site plan) Answer YES or NO [yes]

3

Type of Application

Please tick one box

A This is an outline application ⸱⸱⸱ If so go to Question 4

B This is a reserved matters application ⸱⸱⸱ If so go to Question 4

Outline Application No.

Date of Outline Permission

C This is a full application for:-

(i) Building or engineering operations only ☐

(ii) Change of use without any building or engineering operations at present ☐

(iii) Change of use and building or engineering operations ☑

(iv) Mining operations or waste disposal ☐ Complete additional for

(v) This is an application for renewal of a temporary permission ☐

Application No. of existing permission

(vi) This is an application for removal or variation of a condition of a previous planning permission ☐

Condition No.   Application No.

Now go to Question

4

Outline Applications and Reserved Matters Application

If you have ticked A or B in Question 3, please tick the relevant boxes.
Do you wish to seek approval for any of the following matters as part of this application?   Answer YES or NO ☐

If yes, please tick the relevant box(es).

Siting ☐   Design ☐   External Appearance (including materials) ☐   Means of Access ☐   Landscaping ☐

Example 5.5: A completed page from the planning application form

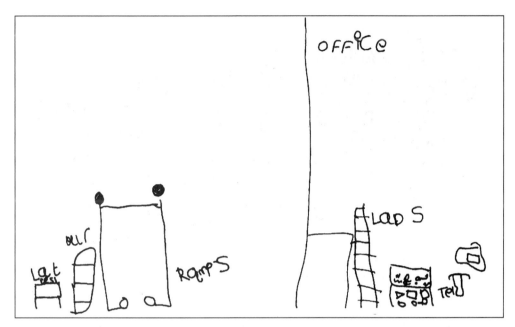

Example 5.6: Plans for the garage and office

Example 5.7: List of things needed to set up a garage (*Oil, car, office, garage, ladder, sign board, sticky tape, tools*)

Some children started to make lists of what they might need to set up the garage (see Examples 5.7 and 5.8) and the teacher suggested that this could be done collaboratively. They were reminded to make use of the list that had been made after the visit. Interestingly, although the children did use the list to jog

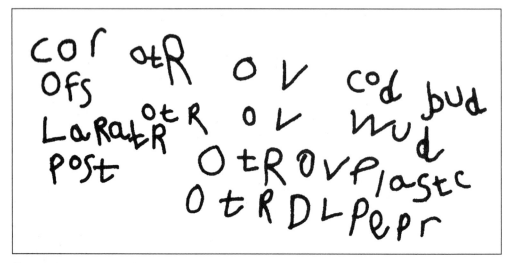

Example 5.8: List of things needed to set up a garage (*Car out of card board, office out of wood, ladder out of plastic, post out of paper*)

their memories, they did not copy the spellings; they were confident in constructing their own. They also considered what various items could be made from.

Several groups of children subsequently worked on making resources for the garage. Oil drums were created, old tools and bits of cars were borrowed from parents and, most important, the car lift was constructed out of cardboard. The office was resourced and slowly the area took shape.

Writing lists provided the chance to use limited writing skill for productive purposes. Lists are often collections of single words and they do not need to be organised in any particular order. Such texts enabled less able writers to use their skills without getting frustrated. The lists of contents were discussed and the kind of environmental print seen on the visit was remembered. Various groups of children created labels and signs (see Example 5.9, 5.10 and 5.11). Each one of these was embedded in considerable talk between children and the adults who helped in the classroom.

Event 2: The letter of complaint

One day we arranged for the following letter to arrive in the classroom.

Dear Mrs Booth's Class,

I have heard that you are going to build a garage. I wish to complain about it. Garages are very noisy, very dirty, and very dangerous. Someone may get hurt with all the cars. I do not think you should be allowed to build a garage.

Yours faithfully,
Mrs Robinson

Example 5.9: Labels

Example 5.10: Signs

Example 5.11: Sign

The letter was opened in front of the whole class. This extract from a transcript of the discussion gives some insight into how the children responded:

T: I don't know if this is a nice letter. If you complain are you saying something nice about our garage?

C: What does it mean about our garage?

T: *Wish to complain about it.* Oh dear! Shall I read the rest of it? *Some one may get hurt with all the cars. I don't think you should be allowed to build the garage. Yours faithfully, Mrs Robinson.* Who's Mrs Robinson?

C: Was it the lady who worked in the office?

C: Yes.

C: It was . . . It was [*several agree*].

T: Oh. It's someone who's got a typewriter . . . Look isn't it? [*shows the typed letter to the children*] Maybe it was her then, I don't know.

The letter was then read again, with the teacher stressing words such as noisy, dirty, dangerous.

C: I know what she's trying . . . I know what she's trying to say . . . We can't build the garage.

T: She's trying to say we can't? I wonder what we should do about this letter?

C: I know, we'd better say we want to build the garage 'cos . . .

C: I know, rip it up and put it in the bin!

C: No.

T: Well, you know I'm a bit worried because . . .

C: Or write a horrible letter.

T: Write a letter to her . . . a horrible letter?

C: Yeah.

C: Mrs Booth, we're not going to build a real garage but a pretend one.

T: Tell her it's only pretend you mean?

C: Yeah.

C: Say we're going to knock her garage down if she doesn't let us build one.

Later some of the children extended what they thought should happen to Mrs Robinson:

C: Smash the cars.

T: Smash who's cars? . . . Smash her cars?

C: Yeah.

T: Julia?

C: Tell her it's not a real garage.

T: Well it's not really . . .

C: You're hanging.

T: Hanging?

C: You're hanging.

T: You're hanging . . . Who's hanging?

C: The lady.

T: You mean hang her! Oh dear!

The teacher tried very hard at this point to bring the children round to a more reasonable point of view. She constantly got the children to think of the consequences of what they suggested, but it was almost as if there was a competition to think of the most awful thing to do to Mrs Robinson. This took over, and it was only when the discussion veered towards getting sent to prison that they decided that it might be better to send a less hostile letter. Even as the conversation moved towards this, individual children still persisted with 'alternative' or 'devious' solutions to the problem. These included resorts to imaginary characters for help . . . setting the Wicked Witch on her . . . phoning the wolf from Letterland. All kind of tricks were suggested: pretending there was no garage being built and pretending there was nobody in if she came to visit.

Seizing on one positive comment from a child, the teacher refocussing attention on the actual letter that could be sent to MrsRobinson. 'What sort of things could we say to make her feel better, because she is obviously a little bit worried?' The children began to offer suggestions about being careful, working quietly, and explaining that things were only pretend.

This reference to things not being real was constantly returned to as a group of children started to work on their letters later in the day. At this point the teacher looked at the letter again, taking each point that Mrs Robinson had mentioned, and got the children to try and think how they could reassure her. And so groups of children went on to compose their letters of response (see Examples 5.12, 5.13 and 5.14).

Example 5.12: Letter of response. (*Dear Mrs Robinson, We won't make a garage we'll make something else*)

Example 5.13: Letter of response. (*Dear Mrs Robinson, We won't get cut*)

Example 5.14: Letter of response. (*Dear Mrs Robinson, We won't have a radio I will not make the car fall on me I won't let the oil go on me please not worry*)

As can be seen from these examples, not all the children were swayed by the discussion.The individual voices still shine through. The teacher used this as a further opportunity to explore audience reaction with the children. If the letters were sent to Mrs Robinson, then she would get conflicting information. This was presented to the children as a problem.

T: There is one problem here, children. We've got a little problem. What is it?

C: What if she goes in?

T: I don't think she even needs to go in the garage, because if I put all these letters on the computer and they all go off to Mrs Robinson . . . What's the matter with these letters?

C: She'll still know.

T: How will she know? . . . What is she going to say when she sees them? . . . Listen to this letter. *'Dear Mrs Robinson, We won't have a radio. I will not make the car fall on me. I will not let the oil go on me. Please don't worry.'* Now that's the truth isn't it? What if Mrs Robinson reads that letter and then she reads, *'We won't have a radio, we won't have a car and we won't build a garage.'*? This one says about playing in the garage and this one says there isn't a garage.

C: She'll have to choose. She'll have to choose which one.

T: Choose which one to . . .

C: Read.

T: No, she might read both of them. No, which one to be . . .

C: Believed.

In spite of what seems like a breakthrough in understanding at this point other children still continued to talk about taking signs down if she came to visit and of trying to trick her into believing that there was no garage.

It was some time before Mrs Robinson replied and in the meantime an episode had occurred (for more detail see later 'grand opening') which influenced her reply. At the opening, Mr Pipe visited the children's garage and, while trying to insert his large frame into their small cardboard garage area, knocked over the model car lift. Mysteriously, Mrs Robinson got to hear about this:

Dear Children,
I am glad you have replied to my letter. One or two of you wrote that you will not be having a garage but I do not believe you because some of the other children said you had made one. Are you trying to kid me?

I am pleased to hear that you will try to make it quiet and clean. I am still not sure about it being safe. I have heard that there was an accident on the opening day. Is that true?

So the problem returns and they now have to deal with being found out. In writing terms they have to respond to an audience reaction to the content of their own letters. Almost in passing, the teacher picked out the word 'replied' as the letter was read to the class. 'It says replied, it must be someone we have written to.' It is important to remember that in discussion the children are learning the vocabulary connected to various kinds of writing as well as how to write in a variety of ways. If nothing else, the children could now see that all the letters were read and the content compared.

To further reassure Mrs Robinson, the children had to come up with an account of the accident that showed it was not serious. In the first instance they had to decide what actually happened. As often happens when an accident is observed by a number of people, various accounts were offered by the children. But they now understood that it was important to make their stories tally. So from a selection of possibilities, such as the car lift fell over, Mr Pipe fell over, Mr Pipe tripped over, the car lift fell on Mr Pipe, the final one was selected. Children who wrote about the accident gave the same information (see Examples 5.15 and 5.16).

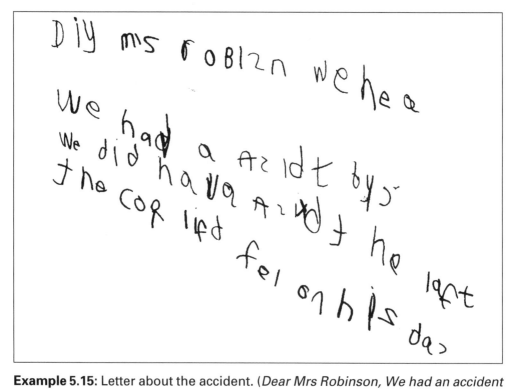

Example 5.15: Letter about the accident. (*Dear Mrs Robinson, We had an accident We did have an accident he laughed the car lift fell on his back*)

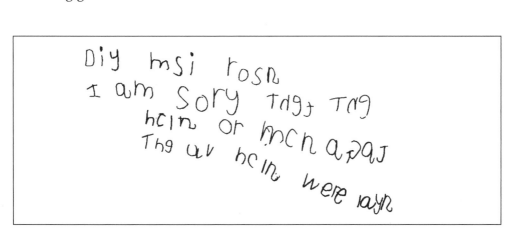

Dear mrs ROBson.
the car LiFD wos meD oF.
PLask and the gorg is meD
OF coReD ana mr pape.
LaFD and we wiL Bc
and I wil Be cand keFLo
wil Be nas and they and I.
a asiDE and we Hau waso
it ih or Bux and we Duho
aisybt Buk Hav
a

Example 5.16: Letter about the accident. (*Dear Mrs Robinson, The car lift was made of plastic and the garage is made of card and Mr Pipe laughed and we will be careful and I will be kind and I will be nice and There was an accident and we have written it in our book and we have an accident book*)

Coping with being 'found out' when writing the previous letters produced more varied responses, and once again this serves as a reminder about the way children respond to moral issues. In Example 5.17 the child took a somewhat holier than thou attitude – it was the others, not her! In Example 5.18 the child was keen to negotiate while in Example 5.19 the child was still not prepared to come clean. Admitting to forgetfulness was as near as he would come to admitting guilt.

Diy msi rosn
I am sory tdgt Tng
hcin or mch apas
Thg uv hcin were layn

Example 5.17: Letter about being found out. (*Dear Mrs Robinson, I am sorry that the children are making a garage the other children were lying*)

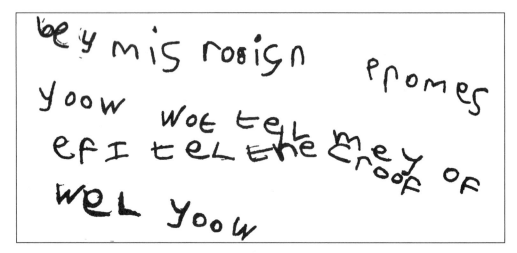

Example 5.18: Letter about being found out. (*Dear Mrs Robinson, Promise you wont tell me off if I tell you the truth Will you?*)

Example 5.19: Letter about being found out. (*Dear Mrs Robinson, I forgot we have got a garage*)

This whole episode presents insight into the children's level of moral development. But it also throws some light on their understanding of how their pieces of writing would be read. The fact that the various responses would be considered alongside each other, the contents compared and contrasted, did not seem to be part of these children's awareness. It seems so obvious to us but even when it was pointed out to them quite explicitly, they were, for the most part, preoccupied with their own way of handling the problem.

Event 3: The grand opening

Given that a considerable amount of effort and time had been spent getting planning permission, drawing plans, writing lists, arguing with Mrs Robinson and building the garage area, it was felt the finishing of the garage needed to be marked by a grand opening.

A number of discussions took place about various aspects of preparing for the opening. One in particular focusing on making a newspaper. Local newspapers often carry announcements about the opening of new businesses and the children studied some examples in preparation for writing their own. One thing the teacher wanted to draw attention to was the way newspapers are laid out. She asked a group of children to examine some writing in one of their books and compare it with that in a newspaper.

T: Just have a look at the front of this newspaper. Can you tell me what's the difference between that and Lee's book, where Lee's written about this. [*Showing real newspaper.*] What's different?

C: Spaces.

T: Well, Lee's used spaces. What about the way it's set out?

C: He's got people watching.

T: Well, that's a picture, isn't it? It's a picture and Lee hasn't got a picture. What about the way the writing is set out?

L: That's round – my writing isn't.

T: What do you mean, it's round?

L: That's going all the way round there.

T: Right. So in a newspaper the writing goes round the picture. We don't usually write like that, do we? We usually write and then do a picture at the bottom or on another page. We don't usually put the picture in the middle and write round it. Anything else you can notice when you look at the writing? What else is different?

C: The writing is small.

T: It's small writing, yes. Why do you think it is small writing?

C: Because . . . because if he does it big we wouldn't be able to fit it on.

T: Is all the writing small?

C: That bit's not, or that, or that [*pointing at headlines and other headings*].

T: So there's lots of different sizes of writing, some of it very big and some of it very small. Why do you think . . . we've got small writing to fit more on, but why is some of it big? Why have they done some of it big?

C: So you can see.

T: So you can see.

C: . . . (?) [Words could not be transcribed.]

T: Oh, right, I see. That's big so you can see it from a long way away.

C: Yes, you'd have to go right near it to see the little writing.

T: Why have they done that? Why have they made that . . . if that was folded up on the shelf . . . why have they made that so big?

C: So you can see.

The children learned about the way newspapers look, the way the text surrounds the pictures, the way the print size varies, and the way headlines are

Grand oPing Party

Thank you for inviting
me to open the
garage I am very
pleased Mrs Sidebottom

10 0   CLoc
Friday 29
JAnuARy 1993

Mr Pipe

garages
Hazel Grove
INfant ScOoL

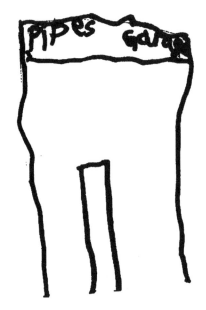

A famus Person
wil cut the ribon
thay will be Sum
drincs and ~ Sum
biscists

Congratufations
to you all from
Mr. Pipe

Congratulations
to Pipe Garage
may you have a
successful time

from Mrs Platt
designer of your
overalls.

Congratulations on your
new garaye from :-
                Mrs Berry

Example 5.20: First page of the newspaper

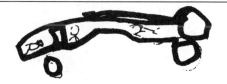

It wil biy clin
and tadi and it
wot biy horbl.
We wil wosh or
haz biyfur wiy
tuch yur cor.
We dw put the tooz
away and we wot brc
yor cors and we wot
let the caz go fruw
the rhf.Wiy wot smash
wiz and wiy wot smash
eny cars.

The peepol hep the
nuv peepol. dey whrk
hod. The ofis peepol
or smaliy.

Hiy wud brus up with
the brus and wosh or
hans.

Example 5.21: Newspaper advertisement for the garage

used for important points. They also had some experience of trying to turn their own statements into headline language. They drafted their ideas and compiled the page in hand-written text. In the process of creating the newspaper they also talked about who could open the garage. This involved them in thinking about the notion of 'Important Person'. Their ideas here ranged from the teacher, Princess Diana, Michael Jackson, to one child who said 'Me, I'm important'. In the end a suitable and available person was found – the head teacher. The children were concerned about the quality of their newspaper:

> C: Mrs Booth, are we going to write a proper newspaper?
> T: We're going to make a newspaper report, yes, for people to read about the garage. OK?
> C: Mrs Booth, are we going to write it on best paper?
> T: On best paper.

Various people were asked to contribute pieces for the front page of the newspaper (see Example 5.20), making a collection of different styles of writing. There is also an advertisement from the garage itself (see Example 5.21) that tells what the garage will be able to do and so persuades the reader to use its services. It reflects discussion about what kinds of services customers might or might not be attracted by.

Further preparation for the opening involved the making of invitations to be sent out to guests; these were mounted on gold card to make them extra special (see Example 5.22). Even this relatively simple writing task called for thought about what to include. The children drew on their experience of party invitations to do this, having in one case to realise that it was not the child's house that needed to be mentioned, but the garage.

The programme of events and badges provided yet other kinds of writing experience (see Examples 5.23 and 5.24).

On the day of the opening the staff had made a special effort to create a sense of occasion. The way to the garage was cordoned off with tape to keep the crowds back. The entrance to the garage had a ribbon waiting to be cut, the band played and the important visitors were shown to their places. The headmistress, complete with hat and bouquet, really did look the part. Visitors included the real Mr Pipe who was eager to see the play garage but, as already

you ar invatit to our grand opning at mr pipes garage at 10 o klok on friday 29th janwery in the morning

Example 5.22: Invitation to the Grand Opening

Program of Evets

Famus person cums to open garage

Cut the ribbon

Fotos teccn

Food and drink

Praz giving

Example 5.23: Programme of events

Example 5.24: Name badge (*Important visitor*)

mentioned, had an unfortunate accident while he was looking round. The cardboard car lift fell on him. Of course this was a very minor problem and generally would have been forgotten about, but just at this time Mrs Robinson was thinking about writing to the children, and we have already seen the resulting correspondence.

A further consequence of the accident was a discussion about what happens when people have accidents at work or, in the children's case, at school. A number of personal experiences were recalled of children who had had bumps that necessitated entries in the school accident book. The reasons why such books were important were thought about and the idea of writing in order to remember things was considered. The teacher showed the children the school accident book, drawing attention to the writing associated with it:

> T: I know this is the accident book even before I open it, how do I know that?
> C: It's got its name on.
> T: Yes, there it says 'Accident Book'.

As they explored the various entries she drew attention to the important details and the fact that dates and names and places and times had been included:

> Let me read it out, '22 *November: Julia Jacobs bumped her ear when she and David Dilby bumped heads in the playground at lunch time'.* So it tells us who and what happened. It tells us how and what time.

The children were very interested in the idea of the book and were especially interested in the entries about people they knew. One entry was about their teacher. They could remember the occasion when the guillotine had fallen on her foot and another teacher had to come and take care of them. The children wanted their own accident book for the garage (see Example 5.25).

time	dayt	ís enˌıee won herʈ	wot Hafond
looclok	29 th January	No	The Lift fell on mr Pipe

Example 5.25: Page from the accident book

In order to produce an accident book for the garage, the children had to consider the best way to record the information. They were encouraged to study a number of forms and see how information could be collected in ways other than continuous text. There was talk of 'dividing it up' and 'using columns'. They also had to decide which way round to use the book in order to find room for each of the headings. The first entry in the accident book the children created for the garage is shown above. As can be seen, the entry is short but to the point. It proved to be another example of writing that was purposeful, could be incorporated as part of the play and which required relatively little effort.

Event 4: Applying for a job

At this point the children began to use the play area. It is also worth noting that one of the mothers made several sets of mechanic's uniforms, each one with Mr Pipe's Garage printed on the back. Thus children were soon strutting around the classroom dressed in their uniforms and hard hats.

It is quite important to note that while every attempt should be made to involve the children in the setting up and resourcing of the area, it is also important not to delay the playing in the area for too long. Children can play even with very few resources and some idea of what is needed may actually arise from the play itself. Preparation should not take so long that the play never gets moving. It is a good opportunity to write some 'Sorry for the inconvenience' notices if play begins before the area is quite finished.

Alongside the play, the teacher introduced another factor derived from the real world of work; the children had to apply for jobs in the garage. Before one can apply for a job there has to be an advertisement. The following example (see Example 5.26) of an advertisement for a secretary in the garage office is one written by a child for this play area. The discussion around the writing of these serves an important function relating to role play. The visit to the garage and the related talk provided a chance to consider who did what and what each job involved. However, creating advertisements also requires careful thought about the detail of each role and about the characteristics needed to do the job. The discussion about deciding what to put in the advert enables everyone to learn about the roles. It is not that the children will have to follow a script when they go to play in the area, but they will be better informed about some of the possibilities. This adds to the richness of the play and increases the level of understanding about the overall theme.

As can be seen, the gender conscious classroom made no mention of a woman

Example 5.26: Advertisement for secretary. (*Wanted A good secretary, must do typing, a good writer, can answer the phone, a hard worker, nice to customers*)

being needed as a secretary, although in the actual garage the office had been populated solely by women. As will be seen in some of the actual applications, both girls and boys freely entered into all the roles in the garage. What may at first sight have been seen as a more masculine-oriented activity was actually an opportunity to challenge conventional role assumptions. In the advertisement for the secretary, many aspects of the job have been considered: typing, writing, answering the phone and having a pleasant manner with customers are all part of the role which it would be useful to know about when playing in the office. In addition, the style of writing adverts has been taken up by the children. A short, sharp and almost telegraphic use of language was used. Further reinforcement of what the roles involve was provided when children chose to apply for the jobs. Remember that not all the children will be doing all the writing activities, so this provides a chance for a different perspective on the roles. It also provides

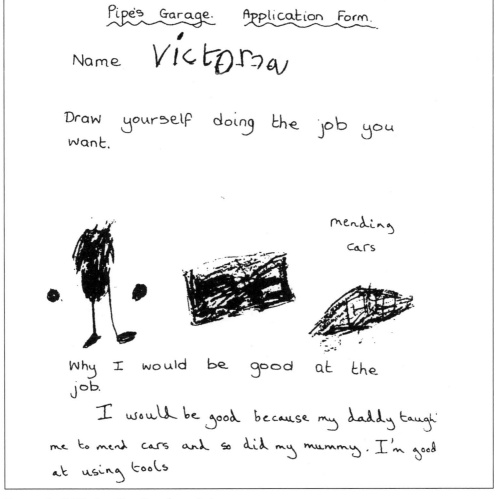

Example 5.27: Application for a job

experience of writing in response to an implicit request for precise information. If the job has particular requirements the applicant needs to say something about them. The children have to read each advert carefully and address each point in their own letters or application forms.

As mentioned already there was a range of writing ability among the children. The teacher was aware that within the activities provided there had to be scope for all levels of ability. In the examples shown so far this variation in ability has not been specifically considered, although there have been differences in the amount written and in competence in both technical skill and composition. The applications for jobs provide a good example of the various levels in this class and how the activity allowed the children to offer their distinctive contributions, regardless of competence. The first example (see

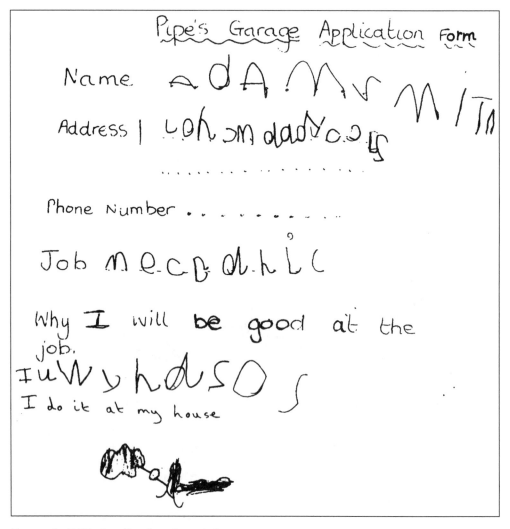

Example 5.28: Application for a job

Example 5.27) shows a child who is at the very beginning of her writing development. She cannot yet write her own name and, on this occasion, is having her thoughts transcribed by the teacher onto the application forms. The second child (see Example 5.28) is just able to use some letters, while the third (see Example 5.29) is already quite competent at putting her message onto paper.

For these different levels of ability to coexist in harmony, without some children feeling inadequate, takes careful consideration on the part of the teacher. The atmosphere within the class has to be one of mutual respect and all attempts have to be given status and shared as contributions to the play area. The children have to recognise each other as learners at different levels along a continuum. This means that developmental stages have to be regarded as valid not only by the teacher but also by the children. (See the discussion later about nursery children's letters.)

Example 5.29: Application for a job (*Cos I can fix cars and I can help and I can wash hands so I won't get the car dirty I will be kind to the people*)

Playing in the garage

All the time these events were happening, the children were taking turns playing in the garage. As with any socio-dramatic play area, individuals interpreted the play as they wished. They chose their roles and played out their ideas in many different ways. Sometimes the play went in directions that had little to do with the carefully structured experiences and it was important for the teacher to allow this to happen. But there were many other times when the free play in the area was clearly based on the ideas developed through the experiences discussed in the groups. Part of this acting in role involved the literacy in those roles and the supply of literacy materials was important in enabling this to happen. Constantly, new notices were added, clipboards were used to make notes of jobs to be done, and letters were written in the office. It is important to remember that not all of these will be fully developed pieces of writing. As we saw in Chapter 3, even children who are very competent writers may, while they play, resort to squiggles to represent words, which they could write properly if they wanted to. We have to remember that it is just pretend after all.

But it is the fact that it is just pretend that makes this kind of play so powerful in allowing the confidence of some children to grow. It is not going to matter, in play, if things don't quite look right. Nobody is going to make you write it out again if you make a mistake (not that this happened in this classroom anyway). So all the children had the chance to write within their roles and to practise the writing skills they were developing elsewhere in the classroom. There follow two further examples of writing created during play (see Examples 5.30 and 5.31).

There were times when the children began play episodes that involved changing wheels or welding parts on cars. Noticing this, the teacher invited some of the players to draw up rules or instructions relating to some of the garage operations. The production of items such as lists of rules and instructions arises more directly out of the play in the area and creates yet more opportunity to discuss what happens in such a place and what the various roles involve. For example, the list of 'Rules for Welding' derives from a clear understanding of what welding is and what is involved when doing it (see Example 5.32). In order to write this, the group of children had to think of what they had seen at Mr Pipe's garage and think carefully about the safety features involved in the activity. But in addition, they would take with them into the play area a more informed view of how to 'be a welder'. In a similar way, the creation of the instructions for changing the wheel also involves experience feeding into the writing, which in turn feeds back into the play (see Example 5.33).

Stock List
─────────

υΥL
aLat testr
gas tester
grıs
tuwt Bud
cor LIFt
Soct

hud cap
tUWL Bos
mast
SPer tAys

Example 5.30: Stockist (*Oil, a light tester, gas tester, grease, tool board, car lift, socket, hub cap, tool box, mask, spare tyres*)

Event 5: The blind lady

Later in the term, the following letter arrived from someone who had a blind friend:

Dear Class 3

I read in the newspaper that you have recently opened a garage. I have a friend who is blind, and when I told her about your garage she wanted to know more about it. I wonder whether some of you could write and describe your garage so I could read the letters to my friend. She would be very interested because she has never been to a garage.

This letter was read to the whole class, as was always the case when letters arrived from outside school. Interestingly, while this was being read the teacher had to stop because of some disturbance at the back of the class. A group of children were pulling faces and generally showing their disapproval. It turned out that they thought the letter was from Mrs Robinson who was not a popular person with this group of children! Once it was established that it was from someone else, the reason for the letter having been sent was

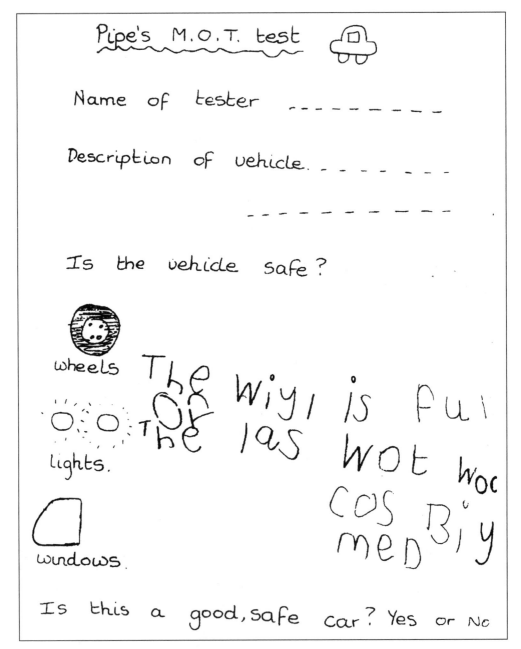

Example 5.31: (*The wheel is falling of, the lights won't work, cost(to) be mended*)

explored. The first thing to be established was that it had been sent on behalf of someone else. Then the teacher asked the children what they could write about the garage. The suggestions started on a very general level with the fact that there was an office in the garage, there was a car lift and so on. The teacher

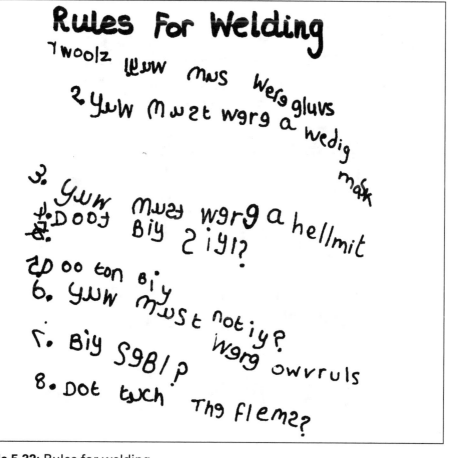

Rules For Welding

1 woolz lluw mws Wefə gluvs

2 Yuw mwzt wɜrg a wedig mafk

3. Yuw mwəɟ wɜrg a hellmit

4. Dooɟ Biy 2 iɣi?

5. Do oo ton Biy

6. Yuw mwst not iy wɜrg owvruls

7. Biy S9Bĺ ?

8. Dot tuch Thə flemz?

Example 5.32: Rules for welding

tried to get the children to understand that they needed to be more specific.

T: If we first wrote 'we've got a car lift' is that going to be enough? If I said to you, 'can you think what a car lift looks like', can you? Do you know what it looks like?

C: I do [*several children*].

T: How do you know?

C: I do 'cos my Dad's shown me.

T: Yes, how do you know? How do you know what the car lift looks like?

C: 'Cos we had to draw it.

T: So how do you know?

C: It's metal.

T: How do you know that?

C: Cos we've looked at it.

T: Yes, because we've looked at it! Can this lady go and look at a car lift?

C: No [*several children*].

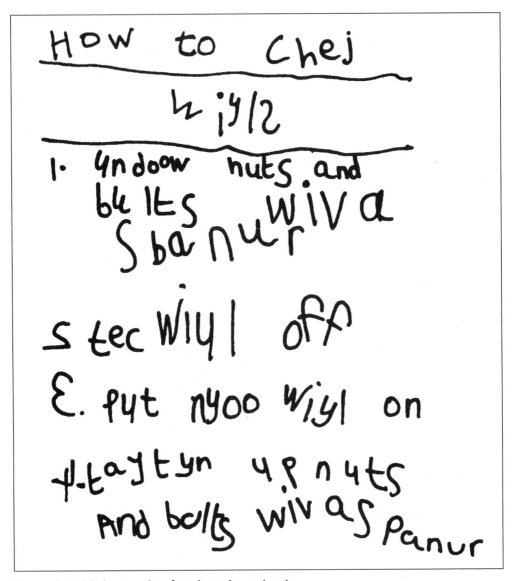

Example 5.33: Instruction for changing wheels

T: So, is it enough just to say?
C: No, because there's more, there's things to make the nuts come off.
T: Well, I just wonder, if you had never seen it, could you imagine what it would be like?
C: I know what it's like.
T: This blind lady, can she see anything?
C: She might have a dog.
T: Well she might . . . What about the dog? Will the dog be able to tell her what it's like?

C: No, but the dog can bark.
C: The dog will be able to say 'Woof, woof'.

In spite of the logic involved here, or perhaps because of it, the teacher decided that the children would need more specific experience of describing before they could manage the task. At this point they moved on to an old familiar activity, describing an object to someone who is blindfolded. This was then turned into a quiz with children writing descriptions of things without mentioning the name. So, what in some classrooms would be an exercise in describing, was here an activity closely related to the on-going play activity.

By the end of the day there were lots of descriptions to read out but, by that time, someone had an idea that would take the descriptions one step further. As the children gathered to share their writing one child said:

C: We could make a blind book.
T: Yes. What do you mean by a blind book?
C: A blind book.
T: What does a blind book have to be like?
C: Black.
T: Can you remember from last year? We did some work on that. We had something on the wall for blind people. What did we make? What did you have to do to the picture?
C: Close your eyes.
C: Feel [*several children*].
T: Feel. Do you remember we made a feely picture of the sea and you could feel what it was like. Maybe we could do something like that for this blind lady.

So a further activity was planned athe children discussed their attempts at describing in the expectation that they would write similar pieces for the feely book, thus taking the activity beyond an exercise or even a game, and turning it into a first drafting of pieces for the book (see Examples 5.34 and 5.35).

Example 5.34: Wording for feely book. (*It is made out of wood*)

IT IS ra n D a n D is on a
is on the Botm a n D It is carG
ROBr a n D it is very me D a n D
cu L is BLak a n D HoD a n D oF
FLor a n D it it 90s the
mot way 905 Fa s on On the
a n D and oh the the
mit it the patn is
or on of Has wiyl trims on th Sigsagy
the tay and the
the tay Sigsagy

Example 5.35: Wording for feely book. (*It is round and is on a car and is on the bottom and it is made of rubber and it is very hard and the colour is black it goes on the floor and it goes fast on the motorway and the pattern is zig zagy and it has wheel trims on the middle of the tyre and the zigzagy are on the tyre*)

The children had been given a very difficult task. When you begin to describe something you invariably turn to something else to use in the description, using the other object as a reference point. It was difficult for the children to understand that any reference points had to be within the comprehension of someone who was blind. Materials and colours presented major problems. The feely book got round this problem to some extent because the children were able to include samples of rubber and they used tin foil to represent metal. They made things out of thick card so that the shapes could be identified by touch. The whole collection of descriptions were put together in a book, the cover of which was made of corrugated card, and letters spelling 'garage' were made from felted paper. The final touch was a recording of the text of the book, on tape, for the blind person to listen to as she turned the pages.

> *This is a welding mask. It is square. It has a gap in the middle and it has a rubber band at the back and the rubber band goes at the back of your head. The welding mask is grey and the rubber band is brown. Three of the tanks that go with the welding mask have gas. The welding mask is big as my face.*
>
> *A hammer has a long stick and the end is metal and the end is oblong. You bang nails in with a hammer. It is nearly as big as my arm.*

Further desptive writing was done by describing the garage itself rather than the separate items within it. Once again, the writing was surrounded by discussion and lots of careful observation before the children began to write. On the whole these descriptions resulted in lists of attributes, as can be seen in Examples 5.36 and 5.37.

Example 5.36: Description of the garage. (*It's got signs it's got a telephone it's got an office it's got a mechanic it's got a wheel it's got some oil it's got a typewriter it's got mechanics it's got mechanics clothes it's got tools*)

Finally, to accompany the book and the descriptions, some children composed and typed a letter about the book, which was to be shared with the blind lady.

Dear Julie

We have made a feely book and we have made it for blind people and your friend has to read it and you have to feel it.

Love from Class 3

This whole episode had provided an interesting experience for the children and had reminded some of them of activities they had been involved in the previous year. It had offered the opportunity to engage in another kind of writing and be helpful at the same time.

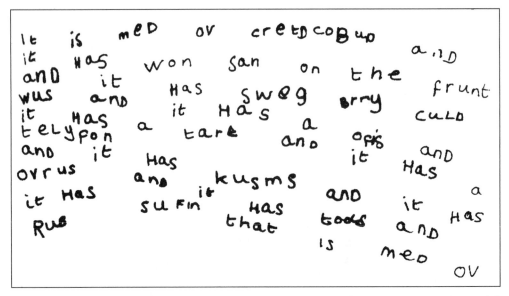

Example 5.37: Description of the garage. (*It is made of corrugated cardboard it has one sign on the front and it has square browny coloured walls and it has an office and it has a typewriter and it has a telephone and it has customers and it has overalls and it has tools and it has something that is made of rubber*)

Event 6: Nursery Bike Repair

As play areas became established in the various classrooms in this school the teachers talked to each other about what was happening and sometimes they decided to get involved in each other's areas. When one of the bikes belonging to the nursery class broke, the staff thought it was a good opportunity to ask the garage for an estimate for a repair. The children in the nursery were encouraged to write letters on their own and then some of them visited the class with the garage and were asked to read their letters to the older children.

The writing was at various levels of development (for one example see 5.38). In spite of this, most of the nursery children could remember what they had written. That is, except Christopher, who said when asked to read his letter, 'I can't read.' His teacher handled the situation by asking him,'What did you think it said in the nursery when we were writing it?' He remembered that it was, 'Please can you mend our wobbly bike.' After being shown round the garage the younger children returned to their own room and the 'garage owners' examined the letters in more detail.

C: They're all scribbly.
T: Well you know when you were in the nursery and when you first came to my class you used to do writing like that.

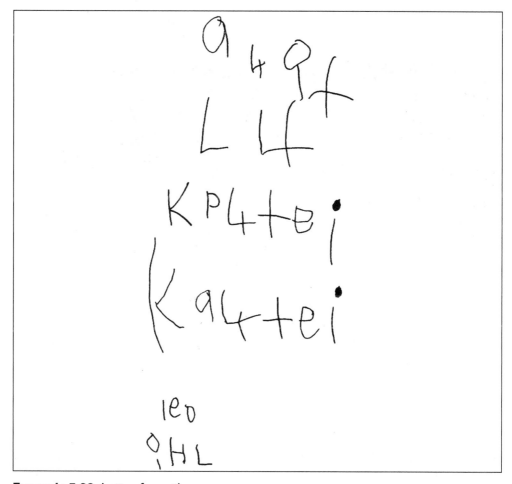

Example 5.38: Letter from the nursery

C: Yes.
T: And this is what small children often write like.

So the teacher took the opportunity to explore with the children some aspects of the development of writing and they were able to get some sense of their own progression as writers.

A group of children were to visit the nursery to examine the bike, but before going they discussed what they were going to do when they got there. There had already been some discussion about 'estimating', looking at broken things and deciding what was wrong with them. They thought they might be able to fix it on the spot and decided to take some tools. They also realised that they may need to test the bike to see what was wrong. It was important to make notes (see Example 5.39) so that they could bring the information back with them to use when producing the estimate; for this they took a clipboard and pencils.

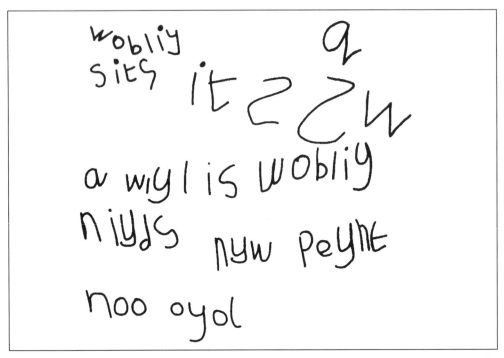

Example 5.39: Clipboard notes. (*Wobbly seat, it squeaks, a wheel is wobbly, needs new paint, new oil*)

On returning to the classroom the children discussed the bike further, drafted their estimates and tried to decide how much to charge for the repairs. A brief but interesting discussion took place, which highlights the dilemma of 'playing for real'. At this age the children had little understanding of the difference between pennies and pounds and had not yet got a clear grasp of the larger numbers. They were aware that the nursery had not much money to pay for the repair. At the same time they also knew quite well that they were pretending, they were not really going to be able to mend the bike.

T: Now you be thinking, don't write it down yet, how much do you think it's going to cost?
C: 20p.
T: Does it cost just pennies in the garage? I know whenever I go to the garage it's pounds and pounds and pounds. It costs pounds to have a car repaired, You've got all the little parts that cost quite a lot of money.
C: How much was it?
T: I think mine might have been about £60.
C: It might be 44p.
C: It's going cost £100.
T: You think it would be £100, do you?
C: No, they haven't got that much.

T: Perhaps we ought to pretend we are a real garage. We could pretend and think what it's going to cost if it was for real.

The compromise was for £44 and a number of children in role as mechanics wrote estimates, one of which was sent to the nursery (see Example 5.40)

The children received the following reply:

To the mechanics,

Forty four pounds is a lot of money. Could you make it cheaper for us?

From The Nursery

In order to take the children's understanding of costs a little further, a small group of children were taken back to the garage by the teacher. Her own car needed to have an MOT (a Ministry of Transport certificate of road worthiness) and she took it to Mr Pipe's garage. When they arrived they discussed why things cost so much to be mended. The conversation, mainly between the teacher and Mr Pipe, covered elementary economics of the cost of materials, having to pay for labour and electricity and needing to make a profit.

T: Where do you think Mr Pipe might get the money from to pay for the electricity and the lights? How will he get the money?

C: From the bank

T: From the bank. Well, how does he get his money in the bank? Where does he get his money from?

C: Someone sends it to him.

Mr P: Oh yes . . . aye, yes, ha ha.

T: Who gives it to him? Who gives Mr Pipe his money?

C: The bank.

T: Well, he has to put it in the bank first. The bank doesn't just give money away.

C: His boss.

Mr P: Ha Ha. I've been doing it wrong all these years.

C: Does he have to pay his customers?

T: Oh, no he doesn't.

Mr P: It feels like it.

C: The customers have to pay Mr Pipe.

Later in the classroom the discussion continued.

T: What does he pay for in the garage?

C: He has to pay for the building.

T: Right, the building.

C: And he has to pay for the lights.

T: The lights and the . . .

C: The equipment in the garage.

FRom The manic

mi pipepag Rage,

The mud gaD Woz woBliy

The Sit it woz woBliy

The Bac woz swican

The agul Baz muvin

The PetWoz cum uf

it nR noooyol on it

itWiL cosd 44Paz foR fisnit

Example 5.40: Estimate for repair. (From *The Mechanic Mr Pipe's Garage, The mud guard was wobbly, The seat it was wobbly, The back was squeaking, The handle bars moving, The paint was coming off, It needs new oil on it, it will cost 44 pounds for fixing it*)

As a result of the visit and the discussion with the real Mr Pipe the children were able to give the nursery some reasons for the high cost of their initial estimates. They were able to explain and justify their charges (see Example 5.41).

Dear mrs Lomes we or sory thet we cont mak the mony mur ceeper it is ExsPentiv becos mr PiPe has got to Pay For the tings for the garage he has to Pay for the tods and the Scroows and the nuts and he terns the ugs on a lettristiy on

Example 5.41: Reasons for cost of estimate. (*Dear Mrs Lomas, We are sorry that we can't make the money more cheaper It is expensive because Mr Pipe has to pay for the things for the garage he has to pay for the tools and the screws and the nuts and he turns the lights on the electricity on*)

The work in the garage was helping the children in many ways, not least in beginning to understand how the world actually works. The discussion about money and payment, while probably not clearing up many misconceptions, was at least able to confront the assumptions of some of the the children about economic facts of life.

Event 7: Closing down

The play continued for around twelve weeks. As the term drew to an end, so the teachers wanted to move the children towards a new play area. Many teachers are very good at setting up play areas: they go on trips and have children make things, just as happened in this classroom. However, most times when the term comes to an end, the children go home for the vacation and when they come back the area has gone, and everything starts again. In this classroom closing down was as important as opening up, and a suitably psychologically satisfying way of closure was sought. Once again a letter was used to engender a resolution.

Dear Class 3

You may have read in the newspaper that there is going to be a lot of building at the airport. This means we need more land and we have decided to build terminal three in your classroom. We will need to knock down your garage. Is that all right? You

could perhaps help with the building and maybe you could visit the airport to get some ideas. Please let us know how you feel about this.

Yours sincerely,
Manchester Airport.

The letter was read and the children were asked if it was all right for the garage to be knocked down.

C: I don't want you to knock the garage down because I like it. I liked mending the cars.

T: So you don't want it to be knocked down.

C: I do. I do.

C   I don't think there'll be enough room.

T: You don't think there's enough room for the airport?

C: We'll have to take the tools back.

C: I like it in there.

T: Do you think the airport can just write to people and say 'We are going to knock your house down' or 'We want to knock your garage down'?

C: They've already got an airport. It's not fair to build another one in our school.

T: That's happened to some people near the airport, or the aeroplanes are coming very near to their houses. What would they say to the airport?

C: Aeroplanes fly near my grandma's house. They're about that big away from her chimney.

T: And why did you not like that?

C: It might have cut it off.

T: Oh, right, you thought the plane was going over very low and it might hit your chimney. When it was near the chimney was it very quiet?

C: No! It was dead loud!

T: So how do you think the people near the airport feel about the noise?

C: Very sad.

T   Do aeroplanes fly in the night?

C: No.

C: Yes.

T: Who's been on an aeroplane in the night?

C: I have.

T: So they do fly at night. What might happen at night?

C: It could fly your house down.

C: It might wake you up.

After further personal experiences were recounted the letter was read again and the word 'decided' was picked out. The fact that the garage closure seemed like a *fait accompli* this time made it seem acceptable to the children. It was also probably the case that after a whole term most of the children were ready to move away from the garage. The teacher suggested that they think of what to write back to the airport. The conversation and the actual replies (see Examples 5.42 and 5.43) are interesting in that they reflect the children's previous experience of opening up the garage. They consider what the airport should be made of, safety aspects and the noise factor.

C: It must be made of cardboard not of bricks.
C: I don't mind as long as it's not too noisy.
C: It's alright to knock the garage down 'cos we want an airport.
C: I don't.
C: I do.
C: Only plastic planes, not metal ones.
C: Right, so no big aeroplanes.

It was almost as if some children were anticipating complaints similar to that sent by Mrs Robinson on the opening of the garage. This time they were being prepared. All except one child, who took great delight in the idea that it would not be quiet (see Example 5.44). Play would be so dull without children like Daniel.

So one area closed down to make way for the next and a new cycle of play and learning began.

The story of the garage has now been told. It was deliberately written so as to give the sense of an on-going, unfolding sequence of events. However, it must be remembered that these events took place alongside all the other activities that happen in busy classrooms. Our focus of attention has been literacy and particularly letter writing, but it could have been elsewhere in the play.

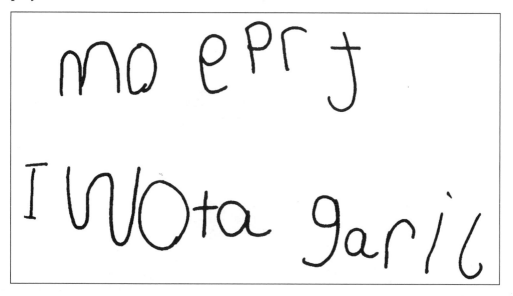

Example 5.42: Letter to the airport. (*Manchester airport. I want a garage*)

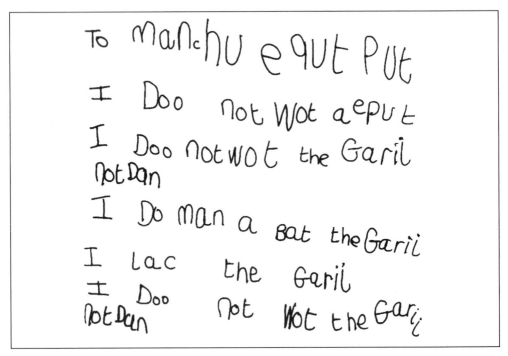

Example 5.43: Letter to the airport. (*To Manchester Airport, I do not want an airport I do not want the garage knocked down I do mind about the garage I like the garage I do not want the garage knocked down*)

Example 5.44: Letter about the proposed airport. (*I want an airport in our classroom I want the garage knocked down I want it to be noisy I want it to be dead loud Love from Daniel*)

Reflections on the case study

It is clear from the case study that the children were provided with interest, enjoyment and a useful learning experience. It was lots of fun for the teachers too. But, as is often the case, being part of an activity, or even writing the story of it, does not always allow one to fully appreciate the extent of opportunity being offered. Yes, the children were involved in a lot of reading and writing; the project was planned with that specifically in mind but, when we finally took stock, everyone was surprised to see just how much scope a single play experience had provided.

Itemising the particular pieces of text, and exploring what the experience of writing each one had provided for the readers and writers, presented us with a quite stunning display of the potential of such areas. We would not claim that every child in the class engaged in every activity directly. Sometimes they would be authoring text, sometimes discussing texts written by their classmates and sometimes listening to or reading texts sent into the class from outsiders. Even so, the total potential experience was impressive. Let us review the range of writing experienced by the children. As some of these were in response to reading events, we have noted some of those here as well. The children:

- wrote advertisements for jobs
- wrote to fill in work application forms
- wrote stock lists
- wrote labels and posters
- created and wrote rules
- created and wrote instructions
- wrote 'thank you' letters
- observed the teacher making notes about visit
- wrote letters asking for planning permission
- wrote when they filled in the planning application form
- read the letter of complaint
- responded with a persuasive text to the letter of complaint
- read the response to their letters
- wrote a reassuring letter
- wrote lists of things needed in the garage
- read the school accident book and designed and wrote in one of their own
- wrote a newspaper
- wrote 'grand opening invitations', a 'programme of events' and 'badges'
- read the letter written on behalf of the blind lady
- wrote a description of the garage for the blind lady
- created a book for the blind lady
- wrote to the blind lady
- read the letter written by the nursery children

- wrote estimates for the repairs to the nursery's bike
- read the response from the nursery
- wrote a letter to justify their repair prices
- read the letter from the airport
- replied giving their views to the airport

This is a very striking list of literacy experiences. There are a number of general comments we can make about it.

1. It represents a lot of writing experience. The play area ran for about twelve weeks and during that time the writing done in association with the garage was only a part of the overall writing experience of the children. There were many other things happening in the classroom as part of the rest of the curriculum and many of those other activities made writing demands upon the children. Nevertheless, even on its own the garage offered the children a considerable amount of meaningful writing experience.

2. It represents experience of a very rich range of text forms. It is difficult to think of how else very young children could have engaged in so many different kinds of texts in such a short period. Too often young children's writing and reading experience in schools can be restricted to story and news (what is termed 'chronological writing'). According to politicians and people in commerce and industry, the kinds of writing most likely to be needed in science, technology, commerce and higher education are less 'story' or 'recount' and more 'procedure', 'report', 'description', 'explanation', 'argument', and generally 'expository texts'. In other words, forms of writing in which the text is not organised in a chronological way. Such writing is often considered more difficult for young children than chronological writing as the text needs to be organised conceptually.

The case study shows us that even very young children can be interested in forms of writing that are very different from either story or news. These more varied kinds of writing are not only the ones that are likely to be highly functional later in life but may well be highly relevant to children's lives outside school. Children these days interact with many forms of print in their everyday lives and writing can empower them to act in powerful ways upon the world outside of school (Collerson 1989; Newkirk 1989). Indeed, in some homes young children may be the only members of a family literate in English and thus have to use writing to relate to many agencies and groups. A number of studies are currently underway in Britain, which may show that young children are very active in their use of print outside of school.

3. Within this range of text types are many that are quite unusual for young children. Few five- and six-year-olds get to fill in planning applications, consider job descriptions, write applications for jobs, create financial estimates

for carrying out work or fill in accident books. Equally, it is unusual for very young children to write persuasive texts, to have to defend something they want dearly, or to instruct others in how to do things.

What is apparent from the case study is that far from putting the children off, these challenges were relished by the children. They had tremendous fun sorting them out and responding appropriately. They brought to the activities a sense of energy, and purpose. It is clearly the case that teachers should not avoid unusual types of writing for young children but should view them as opportunities for children to develop an understanding of many complex events in the world.

4. The activities gave a special role to letter writing. Many of the activities involved letters, either coming in from outside or being written by the children. In some cases a short but on-going correspondence took place. Within the context of the project, and the garage in particular, this was quite deliberate. The experience of using letters this way in this project, and in others, has shown to our satisfaction that letters have the potential for introducing children to a wide variety of written text genres.

As indicated above, many of the kinds of writing in this case study have traditionally been thought by the teachers to be too complex to use with young children. Trying to teach them within a meaningful context would have been much more difficult without the letters being the 'vehicle'. Within the context of a letter many things are possible and, it seems, become much more accessible to young children. What we usually recognise as the form of a letter is simply a skeleton into which different kinds of texts can be inserted. An apology has a different structure from an argument; an argument has a different structure from an explanation; an explanation has a different structure from an application. However, elements of all these structures, and more, are frequently found in letters.

Our previous work with children as young as five suggests that letters provide a meaningful opportunity to explore writing different forms of text (Robinson *et al.* 1990). Our previous research has shown that letter writing is almost always seen as purposeful by young children. If children see an authentic reason for writing then they engage in it with enthusiasm. This is particularly true when the writing involves correspondence, or invokes some response from the reader. For young children it is not so much the writing of the letter but the getting of a reply that makes letter writing so satisfying.

Writing to a correspondent places a burden on the child writer. The child writer has to create texts which have some effect on their reader. The more the children care about their correspondent, the more it becomes important to make meanings clear. It is this effort to clarify meanings that makes letter writing such a powerful opportunity to interest children in more complex forms of writing.

If a correspondent does not understand something, then the writer has to explain; if the correspondent does not know how to do something, then the writer must instruct or direct; if the correspondent does not agree, then the writer has to persuade. Thus the task for the child becomes how to do these things in writing.

These more complex forms of writing are structurally very different from each other, and are very different from 'news' and 'stories'. In learning how to relate to an audience the child writer has to learn lessons that will, when fully developed, enable him/her later in life to construct sustained, coherent and complex forms text.

5. Although learning to write may well have been high on the teacher's agenda, the ways in which the children experienced print were almost always embedded within complex events. The 'complaint' was an event, which needed a written response, but as an event it involved much more than simply the written response. It was a highly complex moral issue. All the invitations, badges, newspapers, etc. were not experienced just as writing but were more powerfully experienced by organising the 'grand opening'. It was the event which was the phenomenological experience of the children. The writing was simply a means to an end; the event provided the end. This is exactly how life is outside school. It is school which usually distances print, and consequently the children, from its purpose. In the garage, children interacted with print in a highly purposeful way and in a way which helped make very clear the relationship between a text and the reasons for its creation. The garage was a context in which certain actions, and these included writing, were appropriate and reasonable.

6. The context of the garage made writing an appropriate behaviour, but it also helped establish the intensity of the children's response. As we said earlier, the writing activities, for the most part, took place outside of the play area. Within the play area the children played as they wished. Thus all the narrative construction outlined in Chapter 2 took place as it does in most other socio-dramatic play situations. However, it was precisely this level of involvement, the degree of commitment, and the sense of authenticity which rendered the outside writing so germane to the play. The play made the writing interesting and the additional knowledge from the writing in turn informed the play. The play and the writing help make each other relevant. Equally, the situation of the play created a sense of context for the writing that made addressing audience and situational needs seem authentic.

7. The garage gave the children a powerful sense of audience. Audience was not simply something implied by a piece of writing; the audience was actually out there and was likely to respond. Nor was the audience simply the teacher as is the case for most children's writing. These were audiences that would respond in different ways. During the course of the experience the children

wrote to several different audiences and these audiences were not all prepared to accept children as children. Mrs Robinson caused controversy with her letter of complaint and the complaint from the nursery about the pricing of repairs resulted in the children having to defend their actions through writing. Too often in school, the teacher is the only audience for children's writing and the institutionalised demand that teachers act as assessors often intrudes upon the freedom teachers have to respond as an audience who really cares about the children's messages. In the case study, the audiences reflected different interests and concerns, and were always fully committed to addressing the message rather than the form of the children's writing.

8. We have already commented that although at first sight the garage as a play area seems a somewhat male-oriented choice, both boys and girls appeared to use the area equally. They all played out a variety of roles. It was as common to see girls being the mechanics as it was to see boys in the office, despite the fact that in the garage they visited, the mechanics were male and office workers female. A check across the writing showed, again, a pretty equal distribution across the writing outside the play. The application form illustrated on p. 95, which so clearly shows real involvement with the process of being a mechanic, was written by a girl. Could it be the case that when an activity is sustained and, perhaps more importantly, opened up in the rich variety of ways as happened in this experience, roles become more accessible to both genders?

9. In this classroom and this school, play was not a second-rate activity. It was seen as central to the curriculum rather than being an add-on which children could use when other more important things were finished. The linking of the work outside of the play with the involvement in the play elevated this experience beyond simply 'doing a project'. This was not a theme in which a range of related items was studied so that displays could be mounted, facts learned, files written and pictures drawn. The significant element here was not simply that there was a relationship between the activities but was the reciprocal nature of the parts. The writing outside of the play had no meaning without the play. Without the play such activities would have become decontextualised, purposeless, and would have had no significance for the children beyond their being yet more teacher-imposed tasks. The play could certainly have existed without the writing but we doubt whether it would have been sustained as long and we certainly feel that the play benefited enormously from the experiences building up through the events taking place outside the play. Despite the whole experience not being a 'project' in the conventional sense, the amount of learning about garages and all the associated learning about events, writing, reading and other areas of knowledge was tremendous.

10. Play is often viewed with suspicion by parents. As was pointed out in

Chapter 1, they often contrast play with work, and play is seen as a less important activity. In this instance, the mutual support between the play and the writing activities meant that parents saw how the play was actually a central and relevant learning experience. Parents, of course, did many of the typical parent things: they made child-sized mechanic's overalls for the children and they came to the grand opening. They also experienced their children continually coming home and talking about the 'events' – the complaints, the blind lady, repairing the nursery's bike, etc. and they knew that these were involving the children in considerable writing experience. The teacher was able to show the parents that the range of activities being covered more than met the demands of the National Curriculum and that the children wrote and read a variety of non-chronological texts. Play, and the related activities, did not get in the way of fulfilling National Curriculum requirements: they actually made it easier to meet the demands.

11. Readers of this chapter will not need to be told that these children were beginning writers. The very fact that we have felt it necessary to provide translations is evidence that the children have a long way to go in mastering many of the skills associated with competence. What, however, is clear to those who take the trouble to look closely at the writing is how there is good evidence that the children are working hard at trying to make sense of what they are learning. Although some pieces are difficult to read at first, with the aid of the translation the ways in which the children are trying to capture their meanings becomes clearer.

Some people may be upset that children should be allowed to write in ways which, at first sight, look so 'incorrect'. Because we have been privileged to work in that school for many years, we have been able to see that the children actually progress very quickly in what are often called the 'basic skills' – handwriting, spelling and punctuation. The school achieves good results in the SATs. Starting like this does not prevent children from progressing. Indeed, we would want to argue very strongly that it is starting like this which actually facilitates progression. Writing is important to these children. They use their writing because they want to get things done. They get a lot of experience of writing meaningfully. This should be compared with so many schools we have seen where children in their first year of school never move beyond doing exercises and copying. But, as we said above, not only have the children working with the garage been getting a lot of writing experience associated with the play but they have continued, in other areas of classroom life, to carry out more written work, some of it of a much more conventional and formal nature. The writing in the case study shows again and again how the children were using the knowledge gained from the other experiences. In turn, the experience of creating the 'garage' texts informed the teacher about what elements could be most usefully and appropriately taught to the children.

Do not forget how young these children were. Some were still four and had started school at the same time as this project started. Some had been in school for two terms, and to some extent these differences in experience can be seen in the performance of the children. Too few children when they start school are offered experiences which help them see writing as a purposeful experience and fewer still are given the opportunity to use incipient writing skills to actually intervene in the world. Learning to write does demand application and effort, but what better way to appreciate what is needed than to engage in situations which encourage you to believe that your writing is important.

There is one other point we want to raise about the notion of 'basic skills'. What exactly is a 'basic' skill? Being able to write neatly and spell correctly are clearly important skills that must develop, but what about knowing how to use one's writing – is that not a basic skill? We are certainly not arguing that the conventional basic skills are unimportant; on the contrary, in the end they contribute highly to written language being understood clearly. But, they are not the only skills that need developing. When we look at the ways in which these children used their writing then we know that at the age of five children can be learning so much more about writing than how to write neatly and how to spell. These children have constantly been faced with the problem of how to create a text that really does something to capture meanings and influence people. Is this not a basic skill? Should it not accompany understanding of the conventional basics rather than be left out completely? We believe this is much more a synthesis of 'skills' than conventional models involving endless spelling and handwriting practice and little else.

To extend our point about the other kinds of fundamental learning about writing, we would like to look at three examples from our case study. In our analysis of the three pieces of writing that follow, we have tried asking questions about how well these young writers meet the needs of the situation, how well suited to the purpose each text is, and whether the needs of the audience have been met. In asking such questions we have been aware that these writers are at the very beginning of their writing experience. We were not expecting to find texts which equated to the adult form. We were merely looking for what could reasonably count as fair attempts by young children and which demonstrated in some way that the children could use sensitivity in written language to address the needs of the situation.

A case for employment

Children wrote applications for jobs by filling in details on an application form and completing a section about why they would be good at the job. The intended audience was the future employer and the purpose was to persuade an employer that the applicant was a suitable person for the post.

I will be good at the job because I can mend cars and I can take wheels off cars and I can take nuts off and I can put bolts on and I can help and I am going to work hard and I am going to wash my hands and I know how to be pleasant

This writer understands that part of the persuasive process is to collect a list of their own attributes that will make them attractive to a potential employer, and these attributes are not general ones but ones specific to the task demands of the occupation. It starts with a powerful premise that she is going to be good at the job but the use of the word 'because' shows she understands that pious statements are not sufficient; they need backing up with evidence. This evidence shows a good general knowledge of the characteristics required for this job. It is demonstrated through the use of simple but appropriate vocabulary. She can even offer more specialist knowledge, as she does when detailing further information about changing the wheel. The shifting tenses are understandable if one assumes that the writer is partly writing about what they can already do and also anticipating what they may also have to do in the future 'if' they are given the job. Of course a more mature writer would make that explicit. The tenor of the writing is appropriately formal in the sense that it does not contain representation of anything other than a distanced relationship. The reader can see that the purpose of the text is to persuade by providing relevant information.

What we have to ask ourselves after reading this text is, does it persuade us? Do we feel that this potential worker has the skills and characteristics needed to fulfil the post in this garage? We want to answer 'yes'. The information provided is concise, relevant and appropriate. Thus, it is a successful, persuasive text.

A letter of reassurance

When the children had finally been found out in their ploy to fool Mrs Robinson about the garage, they wrote their final responses. The letters were to the concerned neighbour and the purpose was to admit and reassure.

We will tell the truth We have got a garage don't worry the lift is not made out of metal it is made out of cardboard. And nothing is real

This is also a text that is written to persuade, but this time the reader needs to have information about a situation rather than a person. Considering the previous letters which lead up to this one, there is also a need to convince the reader that *this time* nothing is being hidden. It is most appropriate, therefore, to make the opening statement. The position from which this letter is written, if not the previous ones, is now made quite clear. It is followed by an unequivocal statement revealing the fact that the garage has been built. Following this immediately with 'don't worry' recognises the need to reassure the reader. In addition, the writer also provides descriptive evidence to provide further reassurance. If this is not enough, the final sentence provides even more evidence to prove the point. In a variety of ways the writer tries to convince the reader that this time everything is above board and is not a cause for concern. It is almost reassurance by repetition. In answer to the question, 'Does it work as a reassuring text?', again, we believe the answer is, by the standards of a young writer, 'yes'.

A letter of explanation

In the episode where the estimate for the repair of the nursery bike proved too costly, some children wrote explanations to the nursery staff and children.

> *We are sorry we can't cost any less and we have to pay our cost and we had to put screws on and off and Mr Pipe has to pay the mechanics and the secretary*

The writer is aware that the audience needs to feel that the cost is inevitable. The writing begins with the apology and is followed by evidence to back up the claim that the cost cannot be reduced. Explanations are characterised by giving reasons and this child certainly does that. The letter explains what had to be done specifically in the case of mending the bike for the nursery and considers more general reasons for the cost such as the price of electricity and the staff's wages.

The shifting tenses are understandable if we consider the stance of the writer. Some activities have been directly experienced, for example, the children played at mending the bike. Other subjects were discussed on the visit to the garage and were not incorporated into the play. This is second hand or reported knowledge rather than direct experience. So while all that is written is in line with explanation some parts seem more within the control of the writer than others. This is perhaps a good example of how providing experience in association with play can help children become familiar with different kinds of writing in meaningful ways. The children could have incorporated into the play the idea of paying wages and paying bills for services such as water and electricity. In that case they would have been explaining from within their own experience rather than merely reporting on what they had heard at the garage. Even so, it seems to work reasonably well as an explanation.

In the three pieces of writing the basic skill we have examined is not spelling or handwriting but the ability to make sense in a given social context. This seems to us to be *the* basic skill. After all, is it not what writing is for!

Conclusion

We listed, above, a number of points which seemed to us to be ones of significance about this case study. We have left until last one vital point.

During the entire course of the case study the children demonstrated massive engagement in, and enjoyment of, the experience. 'Enjoyment' is often frowned upon where both learning and medicine are concerned. Somehow learning which is fun is seen as not real learning, just as medicine has to taste bad to really be doing you good. We utterly disagree! People – all people, not just five-year-old people – learn more efficiently, with greater intensity and with more purpose when the learning is fun. Enjoyment keeps learners going when those moments arrive which require patience, perseverance and application.

Throughout the study, the children engaged in the writing with considerable intensity and purpose. The children were probably not particularly conscious that they were engaged in a learning experience. This was living rather than learning. When someone says you cannot have your garage, you do not stop and think, 'I must learn how to write a reassuring text.' You intuitively call on your knowledge and skill to develop an appropriate response. When the teacher talks about it with you, the conversation helps you think of things you might not have known or had forgotten about. However, when you come to write, you do so not because that is the set exercise but because you want your garage! In the process, a whole range of skills are developed and the result is a more experienced and competent writer.

CHAPTER 6
Conclusion

In Chapter 1 we invited readers to consider the possible relationships between writing and play and showed how relationships between these two areas had developed during recent years. We said that the function of Chapter 1 was to introduce the argument that writing and play have a number of interesting relationships, not to be the argument itself; the whole book was to be our argument. We hope we have now shown that play and literacy do have a number of important possible relationships, all of which are exciting, all of which are meaningful and all of which have immense power for young children's learning.

We hope we have shown that all socio-dramatic play can count as authorship and that authorship does not have to be of the more formal written kind. Young players are instinctive authors as they create their play worlds and we should be drawing on this experience rather than marginalising it by dismissing it as 'only play'. We hope we have also shown that when children are offered facilities for writing within their play, they will often use them. These are almost always used in the pursuit of play, rather than the other way round. The children use them because they are relevant to their needs while playing. Finally, we hope we have shown that the vitality and authenticity of play can spill over from the play and help make other kinds of authoring experiences meaningful and satisfying for young children.

We are not saying that every socio-dramatic play experience in school has to have a formal relationship with writing. There is a danger in a book which highlights the relationships between writing and play that we might seem to be suggesting the exploitation of every play experience to teach children something about authorship. Far from it; our examples are *only* examples of what can happen. They are certainly not prescriptions for every occasion. Play has many benefits apart from those we have discussed in this book and we certainly have a commitment to allowing children to have those private spaces in classrooms where they can play however they wish. We offer possibilities only for those occasions when a sensitive professional judges them to be appropriate and relevant to the needs and interests of the children.

We have concentrated in this book on writing. However, it will be clear to all readers that so much of what we have said, and so many of our examples, involve exploration of the world of literacy as a whole. The case study shows how the activities of reading and writing are mutually supportive. Although our emphasis has been on authorship, children's learning has spanned the whole of literacy. This is how it should be. It would be absurd to talk about writing being contextually embedded in 'events' in ways that somehow excluded reading. What kind of events could they be? – certainly not authentic ones.

It is also important to note that even if we had taken our focus to be on literacy rather than just writing, we would still have ignored the many other areas that feature in a play world constructed around events. We would like to explore one wider issue, and to do so we will draw again on the case study of Chapter 5. We want to consider how the case study opens up children's understanding of the world of work, especially how work is socially situated.

In British early years classrooms any formal experience relating to work usually occurs as part of simple topics with titles such as 'People who help us'. These usually involve children in looking at occupations that have concrete and accessible features – the baker, the police officer, the fire person, the nursing officer, and so on. Typically, the children hear about the occupation, draw pictures and maybe write a story involving a person who helps. Sometimes the person comes into the school and talks about what they do and sometimes the children visit the place where the task is carried out. However, such a topic is virtually always centred around the tasks an individual performs and adult participants are usually concerned to simplify descriptions of tasks in order to make them comprehensible and accessible to such young children. Work then becomes an action a person performs: the baker bakes, the police officer arrests people or directs traffic, the fire person holds a hose and rings a bell, and the nurse takes temperatures.

To some extent this would be true of the garage play experience. The visit to the garage was to see what people did there and certainly the children enjoyed playing at mending cars and repairing tyres and so on. However, there was a quite different experience of work embedded within the events experienced by the children. Take the first event: the planning application.

When the teacher told the children they needed permission, the children naturally first considered the usual source of permissions in schools – teachers and headteachers. They may have been puzzled by the teacher referring them to the Town Hall; what precisely can be the connection between the Town Hall (a place that they have probably never heard of) and their garage? Being obedient children they composed their letters to the Town Hall asking for planning permission and, as we saw earlier, it was a very abstract concept for them, for some the equivalent of asking for bits for their garage.

When the planning form arrived the children were firstly aware that the teacher had not been lying to them, it really was the Town Hall that had jurisdiction over their garage. As they, with the help of the teacher, probed the planning application form (a text-based study if ever there was one) so they were forced to consider some new issues. While the text was arranged formally on the page and was sometimes couched in rather bureaucratic language, most of these issues were well within the comprehension of the children. They were able to answer questions about size by pacing out their area (it went onto the form as '12 fusteps long and 9 wad'), about whether the proposal was for a temporary period and if so for how long, and they were able to describe the previous uses ('a house') and with what the garage was going to be made ('karagated card'). They became aware of some environmental considerations by answering questions about the removal of surface water ('in the sink') and foul sewage ('down the pipe'), and after being warned about the dangers of touching any oil, on their initial visit, were able to document on the form some hazardous substances. They were able to say how many people were going to work in the garage, indicate the opening hours and whether there would be any plant or machinery ('car lift mshin'). Several of the children filled in the forms which were sent back to the Planning Department who quickly gave their permission.

Probably for the first time in their lives these five-year-olds became aware of a notion of authority and regulation that lay outside the family and the school. They began to see that a bureaucracy is involved and that work, and in this instance work places, do not have freedom to exist and do whatever they want. However, at the same time they could see the point of many of the questions. Even five-year-olds these days can appreciate the need for workplaces, especially industrial ones, to have concern for drainage, hazardous substances, etc. In an embryonic way, these very young children were beginning to see how work cannot be decontextualised from the wider world in which it is situated. Even in this relatively simple procedural event, the children have explored a range of texts which, as authentic literacy texts, moved them away from the autonomous nature of school literacy practices and inevitably pulled them into an appreciation of work as more than just a set of individual performances.

The letter of complaint introduced another element related to the social nature of work. In this case work had to have regard to the views and feelings of people in the local community. The children, even before playing in their garage, are realising the conditions that have to be met before any workplace or business can begin operation. More importantly, the children have realised that there is negotiation involved in the process; they were able to engage with the neighbour either to reassure her or, in some cases, blatantly lie to her. The liars, though, were ultimately caught out and had to engage in some retrospective justification. This event also continued to raise the children's sense of health and safety issues in relation to which Mr Pipe's accident proved rather providential. The development of their own accident book, the need to document accidents, and the requirement to be able to explain them and offer reassurances about future conduct, all added to the sense of work and workplaces needing a sense of social responsibility. The children understood that they had obligations to other people and, perhaps more importantly, realised that other people were observing what went on (and for the duration of the project any mention of Mrs Robinson's name brought hostile looks and comments from some of the children).

Consider also how the job application event helped them realise that people in work had job descriptions and to undertake these posts people had to be suitably qualified and be able to fill in application forms. The nursery bike repair event introduced a whole set of issues about work. After their visit to the nursery the mechanics had to draft estimates, the costing of which proved problematic for children with little formal knowledge of money. After a reminder from the nursery about the expensive nature of their quotations, the children had to consider value for money. The children's understanding of the financial and economic aspects of the operation of a garage, and of engaging in a transaction, were considerably extended by the discussion with Mr Pipe, after which point they were able to respond and justify their prices. It is perhaps worth reminding the reader that these were five-year-olds and it can seem extraordinary that such young children could handle all the new concepts and new information. However, they did so comfortably. They seemed to have no problem at all in understanding why the different elements in the process were needed.

Was anything actually learned about work as a socially situated activity? The final event of the garage play, the closing down of the garage, provided some clues. When they responded to the initial letter there were numerous echoes of the earlier issues:

'It is not OK if it is too noisy.'

'Be very quiet.'

'You have to do permission to the Town (Hall).'

'The aeroplanes have to made out of cardboard.'

Clearly, while inexperience may limit the children's understanding, something gets through and is remembered. The event-based nature of children's play, its real-world associations, and clever interventions from a teacher made for powerful, extended and broad experiences of the nature of work. It involved experiences in which the children, using authentic literacy, made choices related to a range of purposes, involved different audiences, handled complex webs of areas of knowledge, and orchestrated equally complex responses. Children may be young, may be inexperienced, and may make less than perfect responses, but that is no excuse to ban them from operating in the world as knowing, active people. Children do not need protecting from real world concepts simply because they do not have complete understanding of them, any more than adults should be protected from using electricity because they do not understand the complexities of its origin and production. Work, where five-year-olds are concerned, does not have to be restricted to simple procedural actions; they can not only cope but thrive on the challenges of developing understandings of work that are more authentic, diverse and elaborate.

That these complex ideas and issues were embedded in events is what is so important. All over the world teachers are under pressure to limit their teaching and concentrate on narrow definitions of skills. We understand why this is happening; it is much easier to assess skills than to evaluate the learning that takes place within complex events. However, we should never forget that the function of schooling is to develop people who can function in the real world. In that 'real' world our experience seldom highlights narrow skills. When we use our skills it is in the experience of dealing with events that involve many components. In events we use our skills as a means to an end rather than as the ends themselves. Sending a get well card is not an excuse to practise our signature; it is part of a complex social process of affirming a special type of relationship with another human being.

The consequence of a tendency to narrow teaching to dealing mainly with 'skills' is that children lose sight of the complexity of events for which skills are required. It is something of a paradox that schooling distances children from life while trying to prepare them for it. What play has to offer is experience of relatively holistic and complex events in which skills return to being means to ends. We are not talking here about only those play events that involve writing in an explicit sense. The kinds of play outlined in Chapter 2 involve many language skills, as well as social ones, all of which are involved in constructing complex play events which for the children have a real sense of purpose and hence authenticity. The word 'authenticity' both here and previously in the book is used to signify that, from the children's perspective, the event for them has reality; it can be believed in, however temporarily, and consequently demands responses that are consistent with reality. That mixture of authenticity, complexity and belief puts skills in their proper place; they aid the solving of problems – they are not the problems themselves.

Of course, not all learning in schools can be of this kind. But that is not a reason for play to be excluded from classrooms altogether. If nothing else, we believe that our chapters have shown how very tangible benefits in knowledge about literacy have resulted from experiences with play.

We have tended to write as if the advantages of relating writing to play were solely for the children. In fact there are some important benefits for teachers. Most importantly, it allows us to see beyond skills to the use of skills. When we watch children at play, when we see them draw upon their knowledge to use writing-related resources, or when we see them respond to initiatives relating to play by reaching for the pencil, then we are privileged to see children's wider knowledge of literacy. As we reported in Chapter 4, on the whole, schooling is not good at helping children understand the true nature of literacy; on the contrary, it often obscures rather than illuminates. Michel (1994) shows, over and over again, that the messages from the instructional practices of classrooms (in this case classrooms in the United States) frequently misinform children about the nature and purpose of literacy. When Amy, in first grade, says: 'I used to think reading was making sense of a story, but now I know it's just letters' we can all shudder at the way school has reshaped her perception of literacy. Michel says, 'Ask a first-grader what reading means, and the first response is generally some sort of task description that describes what is done in reading at school' (p.35). Thus for many children the task serves to define the object, and perceptions move away from a realistic appraisal of literacy towards defining literacy in terms of ritualistic, instructional practices. The responses when asking about writing are no better. Children almost always give answers which pick up on 'writing neatly' or 'spelling correctly'.

If teachers are to see beyond their instructional practices and know how children are making sense of literacy as a whole, then we need to create situations where this wider 'sense' can be made visible. Play is not the only way of doing this (for some other ways, see Hall and Robinson 1995), but it is a particularly powerful way. When children play, teachers have the opportunity to see what children really know about writing and reading. Play should not be an optional extra in early years classrooms. It should not be seen as something beyond the curriculum or something which simply fills space and time. It actually has a role which is integral to achieving many academic aims. It simply looks different from many of the conventional ways of achieving academic aims. It may well be the case that we have to work harder to help parents and politicians understand why it is so important and so powerful. The kind of play and writing relationships we discuss in this book allow teachers to see what kinds of knowledge of writing children already have, allow them to see how children are coping with understanding the world of writing, and offer possibilities for extending children's knowledge of that world.

If writing-related resources are offered sensitively to children within, and in association with, socio-dramatic play then in such situations the relationship between the writing and play is not a general one. On one level play offers a chance to be an author. The addition of literacy-related resources is in no way threatening or inhibitory. On the contrary, such resources seem to open up new ways of using literacy or make legitimate, in school contexts, the knowledge that children already possess about writing. The evidence would appear to show that when given the opportunity with appropriate play situations to reveal literacy behaviour children do demonstrate a commitment to writing, an inquisitiveness about writing, and knowledge about writing. Play can allow both learning about writing and the demonstration of what has already been learned about writing, and the powerful potential of the relationship ought to ensure that young children's classrooms are never without such opportunities.

References

Bagbhan, M. (1984) *Our daughter learns to read and write*. Newark, Del.: International Reading Association.

Barton, D. (1991) 'The social nature of writing', in Barton, D. and Ivanic, R. (eds.) *Writing in the Community*. London: Sage Publications, pp. 1–13.

Barton, D. (1994) *Literacy: an introduction to the ecology of written language*. Oxford: Blackwell.

Barton, D. and Hamilton, M. (1998) *Local Literacies: reading and writing in one community*. London: Routledge.

Barton, D. and Padmore, S. (1991) 'Roles, networks and values in everyday writing', in Barton, D. and Ivanic, R. (eds) *Writing in the Community*. London: Sage Publications, pp. 58–77.

Bessell-Browne, T. (1985) *Literacy play in kindergarten*. Ph.D. Dissertation, University of Oregon.

Bissex, G. (1980) *Gnys at wrk: a child learns to read and write*. Cambridge, Mass.: Harvard University Press.

Blyton, E. (1986) *The Story of My Life*. London: Grafton.

Bruner, J. (1986) 'Play, thought, and language'. *Prospects*, **16**(1), 77–83.

Christie, J. (1991) (ed.) *Play and Early Literacy Development*. New York: State University of New York Press.

Cochran-Smith, M. (1984) *The Making of a Reader*. Norwood, N. J.: Ablex Publishing Corporation.

Collerson, J. (1989) *Writing for Life*. Rozelle, New South Wales: Primary English Teaching Association.

Crago, H. and Crago, M. (1983) *Prelude to Literacy: a pre-school child's encounter with print and story*. Carbondale, Ill.: Southern Illinois University Press.

Daiute, C. (1990) 'The role of play in writing development'. *Research in the Teaching of English*, **24**(1), 4–47.

DES (1989) *The National Curriculum (English)*. London: HMSO.

DES (1990) *English in the National Curriculum 5–16*. London: HMSO.

Dutton, H. (1991) 'Play and writing', in Hall, N. and Abbott, L. (eds) *Play in the Primary Curriculum*. London: Hodder and Stoughton, pp. 45–60.

Dyson, A. H. (1989) *The Multiple Worlds of Child Writers: friends learning to write*. New York: Teachers College Press.

Ferreiro, E. and Teberosky, A. (1983) *Literacy Before Schooling*. London: Heinemann Educational Books.

Finders, M. (1997) *Just Girls: hidden literacies and life in junior high*. New York: Teachers College Press/NCTE .

Fishman, A. (1988) *Amish Literacy*. Portsmouth, N. H.: Heinemann Educational Books.

Forbes, D. and Yablick, G. (1984) 'The organisation of dramatic content in children's fantasy play', in Kennell, F. and Goncu, A. (eds) *Analysis of Children's Play Dialogues*. New directions for child development No. 25. San Francisco: Josey Bass.

Fox, C. (1993) *At the Very Edge of the Forest: the influence of literature on storytelling by children*. London: Cassell.

French, L., Lucariello, J., Seidman, S. and Nelson, K. (1985) 'The influence of discourse content and context on preschoolers' use of language', in Galda, L. and Pellegrini, A. (eds) *Play, Language and Stories*. Norwood, N. J.: Ablex Publishing Corporation, pp.1–28.

Galda, L. and Pellegrini, A. (eds) (1985) *Play, Language and Stories*. Norwood, N.J.: Ablex Publishing Corporation.

Gentile, L and Hoot, J. (1983) 'Kindergarten play: the foundation of reading'. *The Reading Teacher*, **36**(4), 436–9.

Goodman, Y. (1984) 'The development of initial literacy', in Goelman, H., Oberg, G. and Smith, F. (eds) *Awakening to Literacy*. Portsmouth, N. H.: Heinemann Educational Books.

Hall, N. (1987) *The Emergence of Literacy: young children's developing understanding of reading and writing*. London: Hodder and Stoughton.

Hall, N. and Abbott, L. (1991) *Play in the Primary Curriculum*. London: Hodder and Stoughton.

Hall, N. and Robinson, A. (1995) *Looking At Literacy*. London: David Fulton Publishers.

Hall, N. and Robinson, A. (1998) 'Developing young children's understanding of work as a social institution'. *Children's Social and Economic Understanding*, **3**(2), 81–93.

Hall, N., May, E., Moores, J. and Shearer, J. (1987) 'The literate home corner', in Smith, P. (ed.) *Parents and Teachers Together*. London: MacMillan.

Halliday, M. A. K. (1977) *Learning How to Mean: exploration in the development of language*. New York: Elsevier North Holland.

Harste, J., Woodward, V. and Burke, C. (1984) *Language Stories and Literacy Lessons*. Portsmouth, N. H.: Heinemann Educational Books.

Heath, S. B. (1983) *Ways with Words*. Cambridge: Cambridge University Press.

Hubbard, R. (1989) *Authors of Pictures, Draughtsmen of Words*. Portsmouth, N. H.: Heinemann Educational Books.

Isenburg, J. and Jacob, E. (1983) 'Literacy and symbolic play: a review of the literature'. *Childhood Education*, **59**(4), 272–6.

Isenburg, J. and Jacob, E. (1985) 'Playful literacy activities and learning: preliminary observations', in Frost, J. and Sunderlin, S. (eds.) *When Children Play*. Wheaton, Md.: Association for Childhood Education International.

Jacob, E. (1984) 'Learning literacy through play: Puerto Rican kindergarten children', in Goelman, H., Oberg, G. and Smith, F. (eds.) *Awakening to Literacy*. Portsmouth, N. H.: Heinemann Educational Books.

Juliebo, M. (1985) 'The literacy world of five young children', *Reading-Canada-Lecture*, 3(2), 126–36.

Kammler, B. (1984) 'Ponch writes again: a child at play', *Australian Journal of Reading*, 7(2), 61–70.

Kress, G. (1997) *Before Writing: Rethinking the Paths to Literacy*. London: Routledge.

Lancaster, L. (2001) 'Staring at the page: the functions of gaze in a young child's interpretation of symbolic forms'. *Journal of Early Childhood Literacy*, 1:131–52.

Marsh, J. and Millard, E. (2000) *Literacy and Popular Culture*. London: Sage.

Michel, P. (1994) *The Child's View of Reading*. Boston: Allyn and Bacon.

Nell,V. (1988) *Lost in a book*. Newhaven, Conn.: Yale University Press.

Neuman, S. and Roskos, K. (1991) 'Peers as literacy informants: a description of young children's literacy conversations in play. *Early Childhood Research Quarterly*, 6(2), 233–48.

Neuman, S. and Roskos, K. (1992) 'Literacy objects as cultural tools: effects on children's literacy behaviours in play'. *Reading Research Quarterly*, **27**(3), 202–35.

Neuman, S. and Roskos, K. (1993) 'Access to print for children of poverty: differential effects of adult mediation and literacy enriched play settings on environmental and functional print tasks'. *American Journal of Educational Research*, **30**(1) 95–122.

Newkirk, T. (1989) *More than Stories: the Range of Children's Writing*. Portsmouth, N. H.: Heinemann Educational Books.

Pahl, K. (1999) *Transformations: Meaning Making in the Nursery*. Staffordshire: Trentham Books.

Paley, V. (1981) *Wally's Stories*. Cambridge, Mass.: Harvard University Press.

Paley, V. (1984) *Boys and girls: superheroes in the doll's corner*. Chicago: University of Chicago Press.

Paley, V. (1988) *Bad guys don't have birthdays*. Chicago: University of Chicago Press.

Partridge, S. (1988) *Children's free play: what has happened to it?* ERIC Document ED 294 665.

QCA (2000) *Curriculum Guidance for the Foundation Stage*. London: DfEE.

Robinson, A., Crawford, L. and Hall, N. (1990) *'Some day you will no all about me': young children's explorations in the world of letters*. Portsmouth, N. H.: Heinemann Educational Books.

Roskos, K. (1988) 'Literacy at work in play'. *The Reading Teacher*, **41**(6), 562–6.

Roskos, K. (1990) 'A taxonomic view of pretend play activity among 4- and 5–year-old children'. *Early Childhood Research Quarterly*, 5, 495–512.

Roskos, K. and Christie, J. (2000) *Play and literacy in early childhood: research from multiple perspectives*. Mahwah, N. J.: Lawrence Erlbaum Associates.

Roskos, K. and Vukelich, C. (1991) 'Promoting literacy in play'. *Day Care and Early Education*, Fall.

Rothlein, L. and Brett, A. (1984) *Children's, teachers' and parents' perceptions of play*. Unpublished report, University of Miami (ERIC document ED 273 395).

Rowe, D. (1993) *Preschoolers as Authors*. New York: Hampton Press.

Schickedanz, J. (1984) *A study of the literacy events in the homes of six preschoolers*. Paper presented at the National Reading Conference, Florida.

Schrader, C. (1985) *Written language use within the context of young children's symbolic play*, Unpublished report, Emporia University (ERIC document ED 274 466).

Schrader, C. (1989) 'Written language use within the context of young children's symbolic play'. *Early Childhood Research Quarterly*, 4, 225–44.

Scollon, R. and Scollon, B. (1981) *Narrative, Literacy and Face in Interethnic Communication*. Norwood, N. J.: Ablex Publishing Company.

Singer, D. and Singer, J. (1990) *The House of Make-believe: play and the developing imagination*. Cambridge, Mass.: Harvard University Press.

Street, B. (1984) *Literacy in Theory and Practice*. Cambridge: Cambridge University Press.

Street, B. (1995) (ed.) *Social Literacies: critical approaches to literacy in development, ethnography and education*. London: Longman.

Street, B. and Street, J. (1991) 'The schooling of literacy', in Barton, D. and Ivanic, R. (eds.) *Writing in the Community*. London: Sage, pp.143–66.

Taylor, D. (1983) *Family Literacy*. Portsmouth, N. H.: Heinemann Educational Books.

Tizard, B. and Hughes, M. (1984) *Young Children Learning*. London: Fontana Books.

Torrey, J. (1979) 'Reading that comes naturally', in Waller, T. and Mackginnon, G. (eds) *Reading Research: advances in theory and practice*. New York: Academic Press.

Varenne, H. and McDermott, R. (1986) 'Why Sheila can read: structure and indeterminancy in the reproduction of familial literacy', in Shiefflin, B. and Gilmore, P. (eds) *The Acquisition of Literacy: ethnographic perspectives*. Norwood, N. J.: Ablex Publishing Corporation, pp. 188–210.

Voss, M. (1996) *Hidden Literacies: children learning at home and in school*. Portsmouth, N. H.: Heinemann Educational Books.

Wagner, D. (1993) *Literacy, Culture and Development: becoming literate in Morocco*. Cambridge: Cambridge University Press.

Weininger, O. (1988) 'What if and as if': imagination and pretend play in early childhood', in Egan, K. and Nadaner, D. (eds) *Imagination and Education*. Milton Keynes: The Open University Press, pp.141–53.